TERROR WITHIN AND WITHOUT

The John Bowlby Memorial Conference Monographs Series

Other titles in this series:

TERROR WITHIN AND WITHOUT

Attachment and Disintegration: Clinical Work on the Edge

THE JOHN BOWLBY MEMORIAL CONFERENCE MONOGRAPH 2008

Edited by

Judy Yellin and Orit Badouk Epstein

The John Bowlby Memorial Conference Monographs
Series Editor: Kate White

Routledge
Taylor & Francis Group

LONDON AND NEW YORK

First published 2013 by
Karnac Books Ltd.

Published 2018 by Routledge
2 Park Square, Milton Park, Abingdon, Oxon OX14 4RN
711 Third Avenue, New York, NY 10017, USA

Routledge is an imprint of the Taylor & Francis Group, an informa business

British Library Cataloguing in Publication Data

A C.I.P. for this book is available from the British Library

ISBN-13: 9781855756373 (pbk)

Typeset by V Publishing Solutions Pvt Ltd., Chennai, India

CONTENTS

ACKNOWLEDGEMENTS

Thanks to the John Bowlby Memorial Conference 2008 Planning Group: Orit Badouk Epstein, Sarah Benamer, Judith Erskine, Briony Mason, Annie Gerald Webb, Judy Yellin, and Richard Bowlby for their creative work in producing yet another stimulating and groundbreaking conference which has enabled the emergence of this important publication. A special thank you to all the contributors to the conference whose profound, creative, and courageous work can now reach a much wider audience.

Finally, thanks to our 15th John Bowlby Memorial Lecturer 2008, Arietta Slade whose original and vital presentation provided a context for the leading edge clinical discussions emerging out of this conference.

A special thank you to Oliver Rathbone for his continuing belief in the value of publishing these monographs and to Rod Tweedy and his team from Karnac Books for their patience and support in its production and publication.

Kate White
Series Editor, John Bowlby Memorial Conference Monographs

ABOUT THE EDITORS AND CONTRIBUTORS

Shoshi Asheri is a psychotherapist, supervisor, and trainer. She teaches at the Minster Centre for Integrative Psychotherapy and other psycho-therapeutic organisations in the UK and Israel. She was a member of the training director's team at the Chiron Centre for Body Psychotherapy. She is a founding member of the Relational School, UK and a member of its executive committee. A central enquiry in both her teaching and writing is the invisible, implicit, and uncanny bond of connection and disconnection in the intersubjective field with a particular interest in embodiment as a navigating guide in the therapeutic encounter. She has a private practice in London where she works with individuals, couples, and groups.

Orit Badouk Epstein is an attachment-based psychoanalytic psycho-therapist (UKCP registered) and a supervisor working in private prac-tice. She works relationally with all client groups and has a particular interest and passion for working with individuals who have experienced extreme abuse and trauma displaying symptoms of dissociation. Orit is a trustee for the Clinic of Dissociative Studies. She is co-author of the recently published book *Ritual Abuse and Mind Control: the Manipulation of Attachment Needs* (Karnac). She regularly writes articles and film and book reviews and is on the editorial board for the journal *Attachment* and the ESTD newsletter.

Dick Blackwell is a group analyst, family therapist, and organisation consultant. He graduated in business management and has experience in education, alternative community work, community psychotherapy, and suicide prevention. He worked for over twenty years as therapist, supervisor, and co-ordinator of psychotherapists at the Medical Foundation for the Care of Victims of Torture. He is now consultant in group and family psychotherapy at the Baobab Centre for Young Survivors in Exile, and director of the Centre for Psychotherapy and Human Rights. He is author of *Counselling and Psychotherapy with Refugees*, co-author of *Far from the Battle but Still at War: Troubled Refugee Children in School*, and author of various articles and chapters on psychotherapy, politics, and culture. He is associate editor of the journal *Group Analysis*.

Bernice Laschinger had many years of experience in community mental health prior to becoming an attachment-based psychoanalytic psychotherapist. She is a member of The Bowlby Centre, where she is a training therapist and supervisor and has been very involved in the development of the Centre's innovative training curriculum, particularly with the integration of the relational model of psychoanalysis into the course.

Adah Sachs is a UKCP registered attachment-based psychoanalytic psychotherapist and a member of The Bowlby Centre. She has worked for many years with adults and adolescents in psychiatric care, and is a consultant psychotherapist at the Clinic for Dissociative Studies, a specialist NHS provider for the treatment of dissociative disorders. She is also a visiting lecturer and a training supervisor on the MA programme at the Centre for Child Mental Health and at The Bowlby Centre. She has authored many international presentations and publications on the topics of attachment, dissociation, and abuse, including a co-edited book, *Forensic Aspects of Dissociative Identity Disorder* (Sachs & Galton, Karnac, 2008).

Joseph Schwartz was a civil rights worker for the Student Non-violent Coordinating Committee in Hattiesburg, Mississippi in autumn 1964–spring 1965. He is a training therapist and supervisor at The

Bowlby Centre and was the founding editor of *ATTACHMENT: New Directions in Psychotherapy and Relational Psychoanalysis*.

Arietta Slade, PhD, is professor of clinical and developmental psychology at the City University of New York and associate research scientist, Yale Child Study Center. She is on the editorial board of *Attachment and Human Development* and author of numerous publications, including contributing author: *Psychoanalytic Study of the Child, Handbook of Mentalization Based Treatment; Enhancing Early Attachments: Theory, Research, Intervention, and Policy*. She is co-editor: *Mind to Mind: Infant Research, Neuroscience, and Psychoanalysis* (Other Press, in press), and *Children at Play* (O.U.P.). Arietta has also been in private practice for over twenty-five years, working with children and adults.

Judy Yellin trained as an attachment-based psychoanalytic psychotherapist at The Bowlby Centre. She works as a psychotherapist in private practice and is a supervisor, training therapist, and member of the teaching staff at The Bowlby Centre. She also teaches at the Minster Centre & AGIP psychotherapy trainings. Judy is a steering committee member of the Relational School and a member of the International Association for Relational Psychoanalysis and Psychotherapy (IARPP). Judy is an advanced accredited associate of Pink Therapy, an organisation working with gender and sexual diversity, offering affirmative psychotherapy to sexually diverse clients, as well as training for psychotherapists working with the LGBT communities. She is currently particularly interested in issues related to clinical work with trauma and dissociation, and their effects on the development of self.

Attachment and Disintegration: Clinical Work on the Edge

Judy Yellin and Orit Badouk Epstein

The 2008 Bowlby Memorial Conference, "Terror Within and Without, Attachment and Disintegration: Clinical Work on the Edge", constituted the third and final conference in a trilogy of Bowlby conferences that took as their focus the impact of experiences of trauma on attachment and mental health throughout the life cycle. The first two conferences were "Attachment and Trauma" in 2006, and "Shattered States: Disorganised Attachment and Its Repair" in Bowlby's centenary year, 2007. The 2008 conference took as its theme the crucial role of attachment relationships in the modulation of states of fear, and the consequences for the individual, family, community, and nation state when this protective function of attachment fails.

As our 2008 John Bowlby Memorial Lecturer, Arietta Slade (2013), rightly points out in this volume, "At the time that Bowlby began formulating his theory of human attachment, psychoanalysis placed virtually no emphasis on the role of fear and the search for safety in the development of personality and psychopathology" (p. 39).

And, as she goes on to say, notwithstanding the fact that contemporary psychoanalysis has very much become a "relational" theory, the "crucial emphasis" of Bowlby and the other pioneering attachment theorists on fear and its regulation "remains largely unappreciated, even today" (Slade, 2013, pp. 39–40).

This conference, and the resulting monograph, aim to make some contribution towards redressing this under-theorising of the relationship between attachment and states of fear. As clinicians we want to further our understanding of work with adult clients who have experienced massive and cumulative psychic trauma to which there is no possible adaptive response strategy. We want to explore the means by which individuals struggle to cope with exposure to war zones, both in the conditions of large-scale conflicts and societal breakdown, as well as the domestic war zones where adults and children experience violence and sexual abuse. We also seek to further our understanding of how these experiences of trauma may be transmitted intergenerationally as in the examples of the Holocaust and slavery.

Experience shows us that survival, past and present, is a moment by moment struggle; powerful affectual storms often dysregulate and freeze the therapeutic dyad, while disjointed physical enactments offer hints of a hidden narrative. The body and mind of therapist and client alike are possessed by the trauma. It can feel impossible to think in an atmosphere where the dissociated landscapes of the past are recreated. Present reality becomes distorted and denied. Oppressive experiences, disowned by perpetrators, are re-enacted and relived in the analytic space. Client and therapist alike struggle to find meaning and relief from the agony of non-recognition by the other. Creative exploration gives way to compulsion and seeming lack of choice. Feelings of hatred, colonisation, constriction of self and other, threaten to overwhelm.

Re-enactments are at times mutually painful and can feel life-threatening. The struggle for life or death that prevailed historically for the client becomes the currency of the here and now. Madness and sanity become confused in the battle for subjectivity.

These are relationships in which the pressure for survival envelops the therapeutic dyad and takes it to the edge of experience, theoretically and technically, often to the edge of legitimacy in the current psychoanalytic framework. This is work against the odds, where hope perhaps lies both in the capacity of the analytic couple to contain and survive the powerful representations of the client's inner world, and in the possibility of finding recognition and a new experience of relating within a sustaining and long-term attachment relationship.

In times where talk of terror is everywhere, psychotherapists offer a clinical perspective on terror which may translate to the world at large. If we are to find our way towards political integration this will be on the basis of remembering and honouring histories of terror within and without—daring to work at the edge. This work has a mutually healing potential for both client and therapist that engages us in the crucial task of "tikkun olam"[1]—the repair of the shattered world.

In keeping with the conference aims both to connect our own experiences of terror with those of our clients, and to place these experiences within a wider social and political context, the conference opened with Joe Schwartz's personal account of witnessing the terror of American racism during the Civil Rights Movement in the 1950s and 1960s, when as a young activist he was involved in the drive for voter registration in the Deep South.

His powerful piece clearly evoked the feelings of terror in face of communal and state violence and murder, and the essential role of attachments to a freedom movement, to political comrades and to the ability to face down terror in acts of individual and collective courage.

Schwartz's piece viscerally recreates the atmosphere of terror prevailing in the American South during the Civil Rights era, and the personal cost of traumatisation to those who actively took part in the struggle. His piece acts also as an important reminder of the experiences of trauma which we, as therapists, also bring with us to the therapeutic encounter.

In "Intergenerational transmission of massive trauma: the Holocaust", Adah Sachs asks whether the "second (and now third) generation" of the Holocaust can also, in some sense, be considered "survivors". She examines the questions of whether trauma really gets "transmitted" from one generation to the next. And if so, how? In addressing these questions, she identifies the attachment disturbances experienced by the children of survivors, resulting in separation–individuation difficulties in Holocaust survivor families, where the process of emerging from immersion into relatedness is universally impaired. Sachs describes the dissociation, induced both in the victims and in those who come into contact with them by the human incapacity to bear witness to massive psychic trauma, and the debilitating effects of such dissociation upon the lives of survivors subsequent to the trauma. Using the concept of "identification with the aggressor" Sachs explains the introjection by adult victims, under the disintegrating pressures of massive psychic trauma, of their Nazi abusers, who become horrific new "attachment figures". In an important new theoretical understanding of the inter-generational transmission trauma, Sachs suggests that these terrify-ing introjects are passed on to the next generation via an "infanticidal" attachment system. Sach's piece has profound implications not only for those whose lives have been touched by the "death imprint" of the Holocaust, but also for those who have suffered other forms of massive psychic trauma and those therapists who try to help them.

Dick Blackwell too, in his chapter "States of terror and terrorist states: oppression and liberation in political and therapeutic contexts" locates us in the wider context of state violence, drawing on his work with refu-gees who are survivors of political oppression. To the four levels of con-text to be taken account of in work with refugees—political, cultural, interpersonal and intrapsychic—he also adds economic and religious dimensions, drawing timely attention to the economic deprivation suf-fered by refugees in the UK as another source of traumatic stress, as well as to religion as a potential source of comfort and recovery. Blackwell powerfully evokes the different states of mind induced in both clients and therapists in response to experiences of terrorisation, including the ongoing terror in the present posed by the threat of deportation and material poverty, and the importance for therapists of faith and hope in their work as well as attachment bonds with their co-therapists in order for therapeutic teams to survive the work they are doing. In contrast to states of terrorisation, Blackwell also delineates the "terrorist" states that can arise in response to those who are terrorised—with "bystand-ing" as an intermediate state between the two—and which are read-ily identifiable both in individual responses by therapists and helping organisations, scapegoating communal responses by society at large (asylum seekers as scroungers swamping the indigenous populations) and government policies.

Arietta Slade, our John Bowlby Memorial Lecturer in 2008, places fear back at the centre of attachment theory's account of "human moti-vation, development, and psychopathology". In "The place of fear in attachment theory and psychoanalysis" she reminds us of the crucial emphasis placed upon fear and its regulation by Bowlby and the pio-neer attachment theorists such as Ainsworth and Main, and argues that this emphasis "remains largely unappreciated, even today". Slade points out the lacunae in the development of psychoanalysis, giving primacy as it does to the role of internal conflict, but failing to theorise adequately the role of anxiety and fear. She roots this in Freud's own family history of poverty and loss, and his own inability to integrate these experiences into his theory. Slade discusses the clinical implications of assigning primacy to fear and the search for safety in both clinical theory and practice, demonstrating how these insights can inform early clinical interventions with high risk young mothers and their babies. Such interventions, based upon an understanding of the effect of unmodulated fear on the infant's attachment security, offer the possibility of averting, to a significant degree, the intergenerational transmission of disorganised attachment status. In this respect, "understanding, containing, and ... transforming the dynamic functioning of the fear system" is "at the heart of what we do" in the clinical relationship (Slade, pp. 51–52).

Shoshi Asheri's clinical paper beautifully weaves together the conference themes, drawing as it does on her personal history of growing up in a war zone, and on a rich clinical account of the interrelationship between the therapist's and the client's dissociated experiences of trauma. Asheri offers a perspective from body psychotherapy that nevertheless has much to offer to therapists working in modalities that do not include physical touch, and which illustrates incontrovertibly the place of embodied countertransference in relationally oriented and attachment-based psychoanalytic work. Freud's (1912e) axiom that "the analyst must turn his [sic] unconscious like a receptive organ towards the transmitting unconscious of the patient" and "must adjust himself to the patient as a telephone receiver is adjusted to the transmitting microphone" is perhaps given its fullest expression in this type of clinical work, in which the therapist's grasp of the meaning of the client's dissociated experience is mediated through the therapist's receptivity to his or her own bodily responses, and the capacity to track these and translate them into the language of a shared state of mind.

The conference aimed to provide an opportunity to share our experiences of terror states in the consulting room; to explore the multiple survival strategies which are engaged as people struggle to cope with exposure to relational and environmental war zones; to disentangle themes of intergenerational transmission of trauma and terror within an historical and cultural framework; and to connect our own experiences of terror with those of our clients. These papers address crucial questions about how we may appropriately adapt our approach to be inclusive of those who have been seen as "unanalysable", and how the non-verbal aspects of a terrorised person's experience can be safely and effectively worked with therapeutically. These questions have important implications for the therapeutic frame and technique. We hope that this publication will play a part in helping all of us to consider how we might more adequately provide support and legitimacy within the profession for this clinical work on the edge.

Note

1. An early rabbinic Hebrew phrase that means "repairing the world" or "healing and restoring the world", which is a shared responsibility of all human beings.

References

Freud, S. (1912e). Recommendations to physicians practising psychoanalysis. *S. E., 12*: 109–120. London: Hogarth and the Institute of Psycho-Analysis.

Slade, A. (2013). The Place of Fear in Attachment Theory and Psychoanalysis. The John Bowlby Memorial Lecture 2008. In: J. Yellin & O. Badouk Epstein (Eds.), *Terror Within and Without: Attachment and Disintegration: Clinical Work on the Edge*. London: Karnac.

CHAPTER ONE

Attachment theory and the John Bowlby Memorial Lecture 2008: a short history

Bernice Laschinger

This year we mark the fifteenth anniversary of the first John Bowlby Memorial Lecture given by Colin Murray-Parkes on the theme of mourning and loss. That was a fitting recognition of Bowlby's great contribution to the understanding of human grief and sadness, while his clinical observations of separation and loss laid down the foundations of attachment theory.

In the years which have followed, attachment theory, in the words of Cassidy and Shaver (2008, xi), has produced "one of the broadest, most profound and most creative lines of research in 20th-century (and now 21st-century) psychology". Nevertheless, given the hostility of the psychoanalytic establishment to Bowlby's ideas, it has only been in the last two decades, during which there have been dramatic advances in the congruent disciplines of infancy research and relational psychoanalysis, that the clinical relevance of attachment theory has been unquestionably established.

Indeed, it has been the development of its clinical applications, in tandem with its evolving convergence with psychoanalysis and trauma theory, that has been central to our practice at The Bowlby Centre. Looking back, our very early links with Bowlby's work were forged by one of our founders, John Southgate, who had clinical supervision with John

Bowlby. Bowlby's understanding of the nature of human relatedness became primary in our theoretical framework and practice. It contributed directly to our emergence as an attachment-based psychoanalytic centre in 1992.

Last year's John Bowlby Memorial Conference marked the centenary of John Bowlby's birth in 1907. One of the outstanding psychoanalysts of the twentieth century, as a theory builder and reformer, his societal impact and influence on social policy have been greater than that of any other. He has been described by Diamond and Blatt (1999, p. 669) as "the Dickens of psychoanalytic theory": he illuminated the human experiences of attachment and loss as vividly as Dickens represented those of poverty and deprivation.

The origins of Bowlby's work lay in his early work with children displaced through war or institutionalisation. This led him to the conviction that at the heart of traumatic experience lay parental loss and prolonged separation from parents. His landmark report for the World Health Organization, *Maternal Care and Mental Health*, enabled him to establish definitively the primary link between environmental trauma and the disturbed development of children (1952).

With these understandings, he entered the public arena to bring about change in the way childhood suffering was addressed by the adult world. Bowlby's work created a bridge over the chasm between individual and social experience and hence between the personal and the political.

There is congruence between the social and therapeutic perspectives of John Bowlby and those of last year's John Bowlby Memorial Lecturer, Judith Herman, author of *Father Daughter Incest* (2000) and *Trauma and Recovery* (1992). She, too, has directed her life's work to the "restoring of connections" between the private and public worlds in which traumatic experience takes place; but her focus has been on the traumatic experiences that take place in adulthood. She has shown the parallels between private terrors such as rape and domestic violence and public traumas such as political terrorism. Her conceptual framework for psychotherapy with traumatised people points to the major importance of attachment in the empowerment of the survivor. She writes: "Recovery can take place only within the context of relationships; it cannot occur in isolation" (1992, p. 133).

Bowlby had also sought to bridge the chasm between clinician and researcher. His preparedness to leave the closed world of psychoanalysis of his time in order to make links with other disciplines such as animal studies and academic psychology was vital in the building up of attachment theory. The documented and filmed sequence of children's responses to separation in terms of protest, detachment, and despair, as researched by James Robertson, provided evidence of separation anxiety. The impact of these ideas on the development of the care of children in hospital has been enormous. The 2001 John Bowlby Memorial Lecturer, Michael Rutter, discussed institutional care and the role of the state in promoting recovery from neglect and abuse. His lecture was a testament to the continuing relevance of Bowlby's thinking to contemporary social issues.

Although Bowlby joined the British Psychoanalytical Society in the 1930s and received his training from Joan Riviere and Melanie Klein, he became increasingly sceptical of their focus on the inner fantasy life of the child rather than real life experience, and tended towards what would now be termed a relational approach. Thus, in searching for a theory which could explain the anger and distress of separated young children, Bowlby turned to disciplines outside psychoanalysis such as ethology. He became convinced of the relevance of animal and particularly primate behaviour to our understanding of the normal process of attachment. These relational concepts presented a serious challenge to the closed world of psychoanalysis in the 1940s, and earned Bowlby the hostility of his erstwhile colleagues for several decades.

The maintenance of physical proximity by a young animal to a preferred adult is found in a number of animal species. This suggested to Bowlby that attachment behaviour has a survival value, the most likely function of which is that of care and protection, particularly from predators. It is activated by conditions such as sickness, fear and fatigue. Threat of loss leads to anxiety and anger; actual loss to anger and sorrow. When efforts to restore the bond fail, attachment behaviour may diminish, but will persist at an unconscious level and may become reactivated by reminders of the lost adult, or new experiences of loss.

Attachment theory's basic premise is that, from the beginning of life, the baby human has a primary need to establish an emotional bond with a caregiving adult. Attachment is seen as a source of human motivation as fundamental as those of food and sex. Bowlby (1979, p. 129) postulated that "Attachment behaviour is any form of behaviour that results in a person attaining or maintaining proximity to some other preferred and differentiated individual ... While especially evident during early childhood, attachment behaviour is held to characterise human beings from the cradle to the grave".

Attachment theory highlights the importance of mourning in relation to trauma and loss. An understanding of the relevance of this to therapeutic practice was a vital element in the foundation of The Bowlby Centre. The consequences of disturbed and unresolved mourning processes was a theme taken up by Colin Murray Parkes when he gave the first John Bowlby Memorial Lecture in 1993.

Mary Ainsworth, an American psychologist who became Bowlby's lifelong collaborator, established the interconnectedness between attachment behaviour, caregiving in the adult, and exploration in the child. While the child's need to explore, and the need for proximity might seem contradictory, they are in fact complementary. It is the mother's provision of a secure base, to which the child can return after exploration, which enables the development of self-reliance and autonomy. Ainsworth developed the Strange Situation Test for studying individual differences in the attachment patterns of young children. She was able to correlate these to their mother's availability and responsiveness. Her work provided both attachment theory and psychoanalysis with empirical support for some basic premises. This provided the necessary link between attachment concepts and their application to individual experience in a clinical setting.

Over the last two decades the perspective of attachment theory has been greatly extended by the work of Mary Main who was another John Bowlby Memorial Lecturer. She developed the Adult Attachment Interview in order to study the unconscious processes which underlie the behavioural pattern of attachment identified by Mary Ainsworth. Further support came from the perspective of infant observation and developmental psychology developed by yet another John Bowlby Memorial Lecturer, Daniel Stern. The John Bowlby Memorial Lecturer for 2000, Allan Schore, presented important developments in the new field of neuro-psychoanalysis, describing emerging theories of how attachment experiences in early life shape the developing brain.

The links between attachment theory and psychoanalysis have also been developed. Jo Klein, a great supporter of The Bowlby Centre and also a former contributor to the John Bowlby Memorial Conference, has explored these links in psychotherapeutic practice. In particular, the 1998 Bowlby Lecturer, the late Stephen Mitchell, identified a paradigm shift away from drive theory within psychoanalysis. His proposed "relational matrix" links attachment theory to other relational psychoanalytic theories which find so much resonance in the current social and cultural climate. Within this area of convergence, between attachment research and developmental psychoanalysis, the 1999 John Bowlby Memorial Lecturer, Peter Fonagy, has developed the concept of "mentalisation", extending our understanding of the importance of the reflective function, particularly in adversity.

In similar vein, the work of Beatrice Beebe, the 2001 John Bowlby Memorial Lecturer, represents another highly creative development in the unfolding relational narrative of the researcher–clinician dialogue. Her unique research has demonstrated how the parent–infant interaction creates a distinct system organised by mutual influence and regulation which are reproduced in the adult therapeutic relationship.

In the movement to bring the body into the forefront of relational theory and practice, the 2003 John Bowlby Memorial Lecturer, Susie Orbach, has been a leading pioneer. It was the publication of her ground-breaking books, *Fat is a Feminist Issue* (1978) and *Hunger Strike* (1986) which introduced a powerful and influential approach to the study of the body in its social context. Over the last decade, one of her major interests has been the construction of sexuality and bodily experience in the therapeutic relationship.

The 2004 John Bowlby Memorial Lecturer, Jody Messler Davies, has made major contributions to the development of the relational model. Her integration of trauma theory and relational psychoanalysis led to new understandings of the transference–countertranference as a vehicle for expressing traumatic experience (Davies & Frawley, 1994).

Kimberlyn Leary, our John Bowlby Memorial Lecturer in 2005, illuminated the impact of racism on the clinical process. The importance of her contribution lay in her understanding of the transformative potential inherent in the collision of two "racialised subjectivities" in the therapeutic process. She showed the possibility for reparation when both therapist and client break the silence surrounding their difference.

The contribution of the 2006 John Bowlby Memorial Lecturer, Bessel van der Kolk, to the understanding of post-traumatic stress as a developmental trauma disorder has been seminal, (2005). His book, *Psychological Trauma*, was the first to consider the impact of trauma on the entire person, integrating neurobiological, interpersonal, and social perspectives (1987).

Within this tradition of great trauma theorists, the contribution of last year's John Bowlby Memorial Lecturer, Judith Herman, a collaborator of Bessel van der Kolk, has been outstanding. As a teacher, researcher, and clinician, her life's work has been directed to survivors of trauma. Her landmark book, *Trauma and Recovery* (1992) is considered to have changed the way we think about trauma. Bridging the world of war veterans, prisoners of war, and survivors of domestic and sexual abuse, she has shown that psychological trauma can only be understood in a social context.

This year's John Bowlby Memorial Lecturer is Arietta Slade, a widely published clinician, researcher, and teacher. Her work has been enormously significant in the movement to link attachment theory with clinical ideas (1999b, 2008). She has pioneered attachment—based approaches to clinical work with both adults and children, including the development of parental reflective functioning and the relational contexts of play and early symbolisation. There is also a congruence between her current work and the spirit of Bowlby's early clinical observations. She has shifted the therapeutic focus away from the formal categorisation of attachment patterns, to questions about how the attachment system functions to regulate fear and distress within the therapeutic process, significantly where there are "dynamic disruptions".

Arietta Slade's work represents a highly significant development in the application of attachment theory to clinical work (1999a). Following on the work of Main (1994) and Fonagy (1999) she has demonstrated how an attachment-based understanding of the development of representation and affect regulation in the child and his or her mother offers us potentially transformative insights into the nature of the therapeutic process and change.

References

Bowlby, J. (1952). *Maternal Care and Mental Health (2nd edn)*. [World Health Organization: Monograph Series, No. 2.] Geneva, Switzerland: World Health Organization.

Bowlby, J. (1979). *The Making and Breaking of Affectional Bonds*. London: Tavistock.

Cassidy, J. & Shaver, P. (2008). *Handbook of Attachment: Theory, Research and Clinical Applications*. New York: Guilford Press.

Davies, J. M. & Frawley, M. G. (1994). *Treating the Adult Survivor of Childhood Sexual Abuse: A Psychoanalytic Perspective*. New York: Basic.

Diamond, D. & Blatt, S. J. (1999). Prologue to attachment research and psychoanalysis. *Psychoanalytic Inquiry, 19*(5): 424–447.

Fonagy, P. (1999). Psychoanalytic theory from the point of view of attachment theory and research. In: J. Cassidy & P. R. Shaver (Eds.), *Handbook of Attachment Theory and Research*. New York: Guilford Press.

Herman, J. L. (1992). *Trauma and Recovery: The Aftermath of Violence from Domestic Abuse to Political Terror*. New York: Basic.

Herman, J. L. (2000). *Father Daughter Incest*. Cambridge, MA: Harvard University Press.

Main, M. (1994). A move to the level of representation in the study of attachment organization: Implications for psychoanalysis. *Bulletin of the British Psychoanalytical Society*, pp. 1–15.

Orbach, S. (1978). *Fat is a Feminist Issue*. London: Paddington Press.

Orbach, S. (1986). *Hunger Strike, The Anorectic's Struggle as a Metaphor for Our Time*. London: Faber and Faber.

Slade, A. (1999a). Representation, symbolization and affect regulation. *Psychoanalytic Inquiry, 19*: 797–830.

Slade, A. (1999b). Attachment theory and research. In: *Handbook of Attachment: Theory, Research and Clinical Applications* (pp. 575–591). New York: Guilford Press.

Slade, A. (2008). The move from categories to process: Attachment phenomena and clinical evaluation in attachment. *New Directions in Psychotherapy and Relational Psychoanalysis, 2*(1): 89–105.

van der Kolk, B. (1987). *Psychological Trauma*. Washington, DC: American Psychiatric Press.

van der Kolk, B. (2005). Developmental trauma disorder. *Psychiatric Annals, 35*: 5, 401–408.

CHAPTER TWO

A white boy goes to Mississippi

Joseph Schwartz

1. The terror without

At Berkeley in the '50s, where the left wing faculty had been purged in the mess around the loyalty oath, we students campaigned for fair housing against University of California housing officer, Ruth Donnelly, and lost. The Free Speech Movement was to come later. So were radical black representatives Ron Dellums and his successor, Barbara Lee (Democrat, Oakland). Lee was the only member of Congress, following 9/11, to vote against the war in Iraq.

The 1957 Montgomery bus boycott led by Rosa Parks was electrifying. So was the 1960 Greensboro lunch counter sit-in.

In 1961 we heard that Bob Moses had gone to McComb, Mississippi to work on voter registration. Sharp intake of breath. Community organising in Mississippi? Saul Alinsky had done it successfully in Back-of-the-Yards, Chicago. But Mississippi? DeeDee Skinner and I looked at each other: "Jesus Christ. That's brave".

The lynching of black people in America was a fact of life. DeeDee and I were "red diaper babies" (children of communist party members or sympathisers). We knew about it. The frame-up and execution of

Willie McGee in 1951, the lynchings of fourteen-year-old Emmett Till in 1955 in Money, Mississippi and twenty-three-year-old Mack Parker in 1959 in Poplarville were just recent examples that had received national attention. In 1930, the fourteen-year-old James Cameron narrowly escaped being lynched along with two nineteen year olds, Thomas Shipp and Abram Smith in Marion, Indiana. He later described it:

> Thousands of Indianans carrying picks, bats, ax handles, crow-bars, torches, and firearms attacked the Grant County Courthouse, determined to "get those goddamn Niggers". A barrage of rocks shattered the jailhouse windows, sending dozens of frantic inmates in search of cover ... The door was ripped from the wall, and a mob of fifty men beat Thomas Shipp senseless and dragged him into the street ... The dead Shipp was dragged with a rope up to the window bars of the second victim, Abram Smith. For twenty minutes, citizens pushed and shoved for a closer look at the "dead nigger". By the time Abe Smith was hauled out he was equally mutilated. Those who were not close enough to hit him threw rocks and bricks. *Somebody rammed a crowbar through his chest several times in great satisfaction.* Smith was dead by the time the mob dragged him "like a horse" to the courthouse square and hung him from a tree. The lynchers posed for photos under the limb that held the bodies of the two dead men. Then the mob headed back for James Cameron and "mauled him all the way to the courthouse square", shoving and kicking him to the tree, where the lynchers put a hanging rope around his neck. Cameron credited an unidentified woman's voice with silencing the mob and opening a path for his retreat to the county jail and, ultimately, for saving his life "... *After souvenir hunters divvied up the bloodied pants of Abram Smith, his naked lower body was clothed in a Klansman's robe—not unlike the loincloth in traditional depictions of Christ on the cross. Lawrence Beitler, a studio photographer, took this photo. For ten days and nights he printed thousands of copies, which sold for fifty cents apiece".* (James Cameron, *A Time of Terror*, 1994, emphasis added)

The festive vindictive white community atmosphere of these ritualised murders was terrifying. Anything could enrage white southerners.

"Reasons given for black lynching" are quoted by Braziel (1992) as follows:

- Acting suspiciously
- Quarrelling
- Arguing with white man
- Indolence
- Being disreputable
- Being obnoxious
- Insulting white man
- Insulting white woman
- Suing white man
- Conjuring
- Courting white woman
- Testifying against white man
- Living with white woman
- Demanding respect
- Trying to vote
- Eloping with white woman
- Entered white woman's room
- Voodooism
- Voting for wrong party
- Frightening white woman.

(http://www.umass.edu/complit/aclanet/USLynch.html)

Black lives did not count in the US. Lynching was never made illegal. The state of Mississippi was ruled by terror. Bob Moses was risking his life.

Senate apologises over lynchings

The US Senate has apologised for spending decades block-ing efforts to make lynchings and mob violence against black Americans a federal crime. Nearly 5,000 Americans—mostly black males—are documented as having been lynched between 1880 and 1960. Senators repeatedly blocked anti-lynching legislation from being approved by Congress. By making lynching a federal crime, the legislation would have allowed the central US government to prosecute those responsible, and overcome opposition from local police forces, who were often complicit in the crimes. The resolution was proposed by Senator Mary Landrieu, and Senator George Allen, from Virginia, after they read a pictorial history of

racist violence: *Without Sanctuary: Lynching Photography in America*
(news.bbc.co.uk, June 14, 2005).

Following the Montgomery bus boycott, the African American community was on the move. Terror or not, members of the community
were willing to risk their lives to bring down segregation and the rule
of terror.

Martin Luther King tried to explain to the white majority in the country the realities of racism in the United States:

Letter from a Birmingham jail, April 1963:

> Perhaps it is easy for those who have never felt the stinging darts
> of segregation to say "Wait". But when you have seen vicious mobs
> lynch your mothers and fathers at will and drown your sisters and
> brothers at whim; when you have seen hate filled policemen curse,
> kick and even kill your black brothers and sisters, when you see the
> vast majority of your 20 million Negro brothers smothering in an
> airtight cage of poverty ... when you are living constantly at tiptoe
> stance, never quite knowing what to expect next ... then you will
> understand why we find it difficult to wait.

War had been declared on the Southern Way of Life. But no one knew
whether segregation would crack. The tension in the country was
enormous.

Herbert Lee, an activist in Liberty, Mississippi, twenty miles from
McComb, was murdered on September 25, 1961 by E. H. Hurst,
a Mississippi state representative. Hurst was never arrested. In February
1963, Bob Moses, Jimmy Travis, and Randolph Blackwell survived an
assassination attempt when three white men in an unmarked Buick fired
thirteen .45 calibre bullets into their car, seriously wounding Travis.
In June 1963, in Winona, Mississippi, movement activists June Johnson,
Fannie Lou Hamer, Annell Ponder, Euvester Simpson, and Lawrence
Guyot were arrested by police and beaten with gun butts, chains, and
other heavy implements. On June 11, 1963, Medgar Evers, a leading
National Association for the Advancement of Colored People (NAACP)
activist, was assassinated outside his home by Byron de la Beckwith,
a member of the Greenwood White Citizens Council. In December 1963,
in McComb, Eli Jackson, Dennis Jones, and Lula Mae Anderson were
summarily executed in their car. They were not movement activists.

Their murders showed that black lives could be taken with impunity. On April 27, 1964, Lewis Allen, a local activist and witness to Lee's murder was murdered in Liberty. Bob Moses had tried to get John Doar of Kennedy's Justice Department involved. Everyone knew it wouldn't work. J. Edgar Hoover, head of the FBI, was a notorious racist with a book on Kennedy's malfeasance.

Activists in Mississippi were totally unprotected from white terror. The Student Non-Violent Coordinating Committee (SNCC) debated the options. Moses threw his weight behind the idea of a summer project. White volunteers from the North might protect the Movement from the Klan, the White Citizens Councils and the police, all of them the state supported terrorists of the Deep South.

The call went out. An orientation was held in Oxford, Ohio from June 14 to June 27. One thousand volunteers went into Mississippi to work under the leadership of experienced local activists. On June 21, 1964, James Chaney, a Council for Racial Equality (CORE) activist in Meridian, Mississippi, Andy Goodman, a summer volunteer from New York, and Mickey Schwerner, a CORE organiser in Meridian were murdered by the Klan. Goodman and Schwerner were shot once in the heart. Chaney was beaten to death. The coroner said every bone in his body had been broken. Hatred rules okay. During Freedom Summer, thirty-seven African American churches and thirty African American homes or businesses were firebombed or destroyed.

In September 1964, after finishing my degree at Berkeley, I went south to work with SNCC. I didn't feel I had a choice.

Mississippi Burning

In 1988 Alan Parker produced his racist film *Mississippi Burning*, a story of the finding of the bodies of the murdered three, starring Gene Hackman and Willem Dafoe as two white members of the FBI. *Mississippi Burning* is a racist film because it eliminates the leading role of black activists whose courage and skill succeeded in cracking segregation in the Deep South once and for all. J. Edgar Hoover did everything in his power to sabotage the investigation. The FBI was part of the problem, not part of the solution.

The national outcry at the murder of the three caused the Johnson administration to act. Circumventing the FBI, Johnson contrived to have $25,000 offered to an informant who disclosed the locations of the bodies of the three in the now famous earthen dam. Rumour has it that $25,000 wasn't enough and Johnson used the Kennedys' mob connections to have a Mafia hitman stick a pistol in the potential informant's mouth to get him to cough up the locations of the bodies.

An alternative and much-needed counter film is *Freedom Song* (2000), directed by Phil Alden Anderson, starring Danny Glover, a film about the McComb movement. Great.

SNCC's Summer Project strategy worked. White lives had to be risked. Black lives counted for nothing. As Fanny Lee Chaney, a local activist and mother of James Chaney said in 1967: "If it had been my son alone, nothing would have been done. Two white boys were killed, so they did something about the killing of my child who was with them" (Hodgson, 2007).

2. The terror within

In September, I hitched a ride to Chicago, took the Greyhound overnight to Batesville in north-west Mississippi for an orientation for new volunteers. I arrived mid-morning to a deserted outdoor bus station save for a few good ol' boys sitting on benches drinking whisky and rye.

I looked exactly like what I was—Yankee-Jew coming south to cause trouble. They were looking me over. In my head, I could see them approaching me: "Whatcha doin' here boy?" After ten minutes, there were fewer good ol' boys in sight. If they had gone to get friends I could be disappeared without a trace. Scared.

After twenty minutes an SNCC car came screeching up.

"You, Joe? Get in. Sorry. We forgot".

* * *

Women understand the vulnerability of being alone on a city street. Two women are murdered a week in Britain. No matter what happens it's always the woman's fault.

* * *

Although I grew up in tough Los Angeles neighbourhoods where you had to fight, Mississippi was something else. Whatever happened would be my fault. I shouldn't have been there—"jes' makes folks mad, is all". For the first time I had become a target of hatred.

James Baldwin wrote in *Notes of a Native Son* (1955) that when he was growing up he knew about discrimination but he didn't believe anyone would discriminate against *him*. Until he was violently ejected from a New Jersey bar.

Black people in the Deep South lived in a state of terror. After I had been in Hattiesburg for a while, I asked Gracie Hawthorn, a local high school activist, why she thought white people in the South were like that. She said: "Because they hate us". At the time I didn't quite understand this.

SNCC chose to take on Mississippi because to crack segregation in Mississippi would open up the entire South. And it did. But the murder of Michael Griffith in Howard Beach, New York in 1986 showed white America that a black person could still be killed at whim anywhere in the US. The vicious beating of Rodney King by the Los Angeles police in 1991 showed that racial hatred was alive and well in police forces in the US.

Years later at a thirty year reunion, I asked Peggy Connor, the town beautician, one of the leaders of the Hattiesburg movement, how she managed the fear of being politically active. She said, "Oh, the movement was so much better. Before, you died for nothing".

* * *

The SNCC people who oriented us in Batesville were Free Speech Movement veterans. It showed in lined faces, fatigue, and a quiet sense of maturity. They spoke in reverent tones about the courage of local activists: Fannie Lou Hamer nearly beaten to death in Winona; Herbert Lee murdered in Liberty; and E. W. Steptoe and armed resistance in McComb. I watched and tried to learn.

We were taught how to survive a beating, how to protect a co-worker who was being beaten—you lie across them and absorb the blows—and most of all, when to keep your mouth shut. No one talked about fear. Stokely Carmichael was a fantastically good speaker and a fantastically good dancer. Penny Patch's soft southern accent held the orientation together. We were being prepared for the front.

* * *

After two weeks "in the State", you felt very little. The fear was like the force of gravity—everywhere—so you didn't notice it much. If you had to drive in an integrated car—to be avoided whenever possible—Mississippi motorists would pass us on the highway screaming and gesticulating with their middle fingers. The evening anonymous phone calls to the SNCC office on Mobile Street were background noise—"We're gonna get you and your motherfuckin' nigger lovers tonight", Mrs. Woods, the owner of the SNCC storefront office would say, "Don't you pay those dumb peckerwoods no mind". Mrs. Woods made us white boys climb up on her roof to collect fallen pecans. You did not argue with Mrs. Woods. Southern pecan pie is very good.

I lived with Celia Johnson, aged eighty, down on Fairley Street just off East 7th, a fifteen minute walk from the SNCC office. Dirt roads. Mrs. Johnson risked having her house burned down by agreeing to house SNCC workers. She was protected to some extent by having been nanny to the children of a rich Hattiesburg family. Holidays in Cuba, that sort of thing. She made us breakfast every morning, hominy grits and eggs, toast, sometimes bacon. I liked it. Dick Landerman, my roommate hated it. Dick was a first rate community organiser. The rest of us white folks were amateurs. I asked him how he did it. He said, you just hang out. Yeah. It's easy when you know how.

We took our evening meals at Mr Moody's Green Door café. I liked his smothered pork chops served with greens and grits. He gave us workers a discount. The juke box played Percy Sledge, Rufus Thomas, Otis Redding.

A lot of us took a leave of absence to go home for Christmas. It was a relief to be back with my people in the Bay Area. We went out, saw the San Francisco Mime Troupe, ate in Chinatown. We talked and talked. Nobody could understand why I was going back. I didn't feel I had left.

I flew to New Orleans. Took the airport bus to the Greyhound terminal for a bus to Hattiesburg. Two hours to kill. I went for a walk to check out a bit of New Orleans.

I had my first-ever anxiety attack. I didn't know what it was. Stomach churning, limbs shaking, couldn't breathe. I sat down on a bus stop bench.. Scared out of my wits. It passed. I felt a bit better.

I re-entered the State. The Mississippi Challenge had failed: the segregated white Democratic Party delegation had been seated at the Democratic National Convention instead of the delegation from the Mississippi Freedom Democratic Party (MFDP). Lyndon Johnson had tried to broker a deal. The MFDP was offered two seats at the convention.

Fannie Lou Hamer, leader of the delegation said: "We didn't come all this way for no two seats".

The Summer Project was in trouble. Voter registration was still meaningful but had lost its edge. Someone had the idea of integrating the Holiday Inn out on US Highway 49. Four of us—two white, two black—went out and registered. We stayed in adjoining rooms until midnight, decided it was too risky to spend the night and left.

The project voted to do a sit-in in downtown Hattiesburg at Lea's Diner. We were chased out by a posse of white men wielding axe handles, saved from serious beatings by people calling out from the street: "Don't hit them, don't hit them".

One night, I drove the SNCC car towards home to Mrs. Johnson's house. On East 7th Street just before turning into Fairley Street I was pulled over by Hattiesburg police. Two officers of the law got out.

"Whatcha got in the trunk, boy? Open it up".

I got out and opened it. Movement literature was stacked in boxes.

"You know, boy, white dogs and black dogs don't mix".

I said: "People aren't dogs".

I found myself lying on the ground.

I think I was slugged in the stomach.

I didn't feel a thing.

The law drove off.

I drove back to the office, and reported the incident. Gracie Hawthorne got on the Wide Area Telephone Service (WATS) line and reported it to Atlanta. I drove back to Mrs. Johnson's and went to bed.

A month later I left the State. Two months later, in therapy I was having nightmares about police breaking the bridge of my nose with a karate chop and shoving the broken bone up into my brain, killing me.

Two years later, in 1966, the Hattiesburg movement cracked segregation in Hattiesburg once and for all with a general strike. Vernon Dahmer, NAACP head in Hattiesburg was murdered on January 10, 1966. His killer Sam Bowers of the Ku Klux Klan was convicted in 1998, thirty-two years later (McVeigh, 2009).

* * *

I went to New York to look for a job, to get away from the West Coast. I stayed with an old family friend in the Bronx, looked up Berkeley people who had moved to New York, walked the streets of Manhattan trying to reconnect to places that I had left as a five year old, trying to figure out what happened. I started to hallucinate—the buildings seemed to be falling towards me. I had the nightmares. I entered psychoanalysis with Milton Ehrlich, a Sullivanian interpersonalist. I had PTSD. War trauma. The pain was excruciating.

3. The terror within and the terror without

My Mississippi experience of living with terror has left me with deep concerns about the cost and causes of terror. Ultimately terror cannot exist without the active support or passive permission of the state. Racism cannot exist unless one group has power, ultimately state power, over another. So it was in Mississippi.

What does it say about us that no woman can walk the streets at night without fear of attack?

References

Anon. (2005). Senate apologises over lynchings. news.bbc.co.uk. June 14.

Baldwin, J. (1955). *Notes of a Native Son*. Boston: Beacon Press.

Braziel, J. E. (1992). *A History of Lynching in the United States*. Chicago: University of Illinois Press. www.umass.edu/complit/aclanet/USLynch.html

Cameron, J. (1994). *A Time of Terror: A Survivor's Story*. Halethorpe, MD: Black Classics Press.

Hodgson, G. (2007). Fannie Lee Chaney. [Obituary.] *The Guardian*, May 29.

King, M. L. (1963). Letter from a Birmingham jail: *Liberation: An Independent Monthly*, June, 23: 10–16.

McVeigh, R. (2009). *The Rise of the Ku Klux Klan: Right-wing Movements and National Politics Organizations*. Minneapolis, MN: University of Minnesota Press.

Parker, A. (1988). *Mississippi Burning*, director, Alan Parker. Orion Pictures.

Resources

Books

Allen, J., Als, H., Lewis, J. & Litwack, L. F. (2008). *Without Sanctuary: Lynching Photography in America*. Santa Fe, NM: Twin Palms.

Bullard, S. (1993). *Free at Last: A History of the Civil Rights Movement and Those Who Died in the Struggle*. New York: Oxford University Press.

Freud, S. (1919d). Introduction to psycho-analysis and the war neuroses. *S. E., 17*: pp. 205–210. London: Hogarth.

Lyon, D. (1992). *Memories of the Southern Civil Rights Movement*. London: University of North Carolina Press.

Marable, M., Mullings, L. & Spencer-Wood, S. (2006). *Freedom: A Monumental Visual Record of African American History Since the 19th-century*. London: Phaidon Press.

Payne, C. M. (1995). *I've Got the Light of Freedom*. Berkeley, CA: University of California Press.

Turner, J., Stanton, B., Vahala, M. & Williams, R. (1982). *The Ku Klux Klan, a History of Racism and Violence*. Montgomery, AL: Klanwatch, a project of The Southern Poverty Law Center.

Films

Easy Rider (1969), starring Peter Fonda, Dennis Hopper and Jack Nicholson, dir. Dennis Hopper. Columbia Pictures. The assassination of the characters played by Fonda, Hopper and Nicholson shows the hatred in the heart of America.

Freedom Song (2000), starring Danny Glover, dir. Phil Alden Robinson, music by Sweet Honey in the Rock. tnt.tv, warnervideo.com. The much needed counter film to Alan Parker's racist *Mississippi Burning*.

Rosewood (1997), starring Ving Rhames and Jon Voigt, dir. John Singleton, Warner Bros. An American pogrom, south Florida, 1923.

Songs

Holliday, Billie (1939). *Strange Fruit*. New York: Commodore. "Southern trees bear a strange fruit/Blood on the leaves and blood at the roots". Available at www.ladyday.net (see Strange Fruit, Wikipedia.)

Simone, Nina (1964). *Mississippi Goddam*. New York, March 21 live session at Carnegie Hall. Bobby Hamilton, drums; Lisle Atkinson, bass; Rudy Stevenson, guitar, flute; Nina Simone, vocal, piano. "Alabama's gotten me so upset/ Tennessee made me lose my rest/ And everybody knows about Mississippi goddam".

Other resources

Anon. (2005). Senate apologises over lynchings. news.bbc.co.uk, June 14. The US Senate has apologised for spending decades blocking efforts to make lynchings and mob violence against black Americans a federal *crime*. Nearly 5,000 Americans—mostly black males—are documented as having been lynched between 1880 and 1960. Senators repeatedly blocked anti-lynching legislation from being approved by Congress. By making lynching a federal crime, the legislation would have allowed the central US government to prosecute those responsible, and overcome opposition from local police forces, who were often complicit in the crimes. The resolution was proposed by Senators Mary Landrieu and George Allen, from Virginia, after they read a pictorial history of racist violence: *Without Sanctuary: Lynching Photography* in America.

Ku Klux Klan. www.wikipedia.org. Accurate and thorough.

CHAPTER THREE

Intergenerational transmission of massive trauma: the Holocaust

Adah Sachs

> My baby was born ill and lacerated
> And tiny as the palm of my hand.
> And when he cried, grandpa told me to nurse him,
> my little baby,
> only his lips weren't sick.
> My little baby was born ill and wounded:
> I've always known, something
> is sick
> inside me, someone
> dead.
>
> —*Anon.*, poem by a second-generation Holocaust survivor, 1985

Ruben, fifty-four, is a famous chef and a "wild character". He is obese, a heavy smoker, and a reckless driver. Despite his high earnings, he is often in debt. He is twice divorced.

Gabriel, aged fifty-five, still lives with his parents. He is single, and has a very promiscuous lifestyle "on principle" (to use his own words).

Daphna, fifty-two, is an unusually beautiful woman. She is a consultant at a teaching hospital, specialising in HIV and AIDS. She is a single mum.

David, a bright man of fifty-five, is chronically unsuccessful at his work. He is single.

Lea and Josh, forty-eight, are married and have three children. They both suffer from depression, and largely depend on the help of their ageing parents to support their family.

Naomi, aged forty-eight, is a senior scientist, and had gained her PhD at the age of twenty-eight. She is happily married, has three children and a beautiful home. She and her family spend a lot of the time living abroad.

Josepha, fifty, had lost her four-month-old baby in a car crash, due to her own reckless driving (Kogan, 1995).

Isaac, fifty, had shot and wounded his father, during the latter's attempt to save him from suicide (Kogan, 1995).

Kim, aged thirty-eight, is a successful photographer. She loves her work and her lifestyle, which involves frequent travel to exotic locations. She is highly sociable, charming, and warm. She is single, and states that she "could never settle down".

* * *

These little snippets appear totally unrelated. Indeed, these people are very different from one another. Some are high-flyers and some unsuccessful; some have families and children and some never managed a relationship; some travel a lot and some have never left home. Some suffer depression and have even attempted suicide; one was responsible for the death of her baby; and some of them lead rather happy and creative lives. The one visible link between them is that they are all quite close in age: they are all part of a group known as "the second generation of Holocaust survivors". One of them, the thirty-eight-year-old Kim, is from the "third generation". It was her grandmother who was a survivor.

The name, "second generation Holocaust survivors", suggests that these people are a distinct group, and that the Holocaust plays a significant role in their lives; in fact, it suggests that they themselves are some sort of survivors. But is that really so? They were not even born during World War II, and have certainly not endured any of its horrors.

They all grew up in free countries, in at least moderate material comfort, and most of them still have two caring parents. Yet the name "second generation" arose somehow, and stuck. As though there *was* something distinct and different about this group; as though they do, somehow, carry their parents' trauma; as though the parental trauma has somehow been transmitted to their offspring.

In this chapter, I would like to look closely at the notion of "trauma transmission". I will ask, and try to answer, two related questions. Does trauma really get "transmitted"? And if so, how, exactly, does that happen?

Intuitively, it seems quite plausible that growing up with traumatised parents may be traumatising for their children. But is this the same actual trauma being "transmitted", or the consequences of a painful upbringing?

In some cases, like, for example, violent families, there may be an apparently obvious "transmission pathway", through the repetition of the same kind of violent behaviour that the now adult child suffered, being directed towards his or her own children. Each generation, in turn, thus experiences the same type of trauma. I would like to suggest, however, that even in those families where obviously dysfunctional behaviour is inflicted down the generations, the most traumatising element is not the violent behaviour itself but something else, which is even more powerful than that behaviour, and yet may be completely invisible.

The offspring of Holocaust survivors, at any rate, have had a completely different experience to that of their parents. For one, they have not lived through the Holocaust. Furthermore, their parents, the survivors, are on the whole highly protective and caring parents, who rarely manifest abusive behaviour towards their children. They are, generally, a well-adjusted population. Most of them have families, homes, jobs; they go on holidays and do not seem to act in strange ways. In their homes, most of them avoid even mentioning the Holocaust. It is not easy to see what exactly may cause trauma in their offspring. And yet, organisations that, forty years ago, offered support and therapy to Holocaust survivors, are now finding their hands full with the second and even third generations of these survivors. The poem quoted at the beginning of this paper was not written by a survivor, but by a daughter of one; and she writes about her sense of damage to her own baby, a "third generation survivor". The trauma seems to continue to unfold, somehow, generation after generation.

Many researchers have tried to compare the "second generation" group to controls, regarding their levels of happiness, capacity for intimacy, sexuality, procreation, ambition and achievement, delinquency, psychiatric disturbance, individuation, depression, and attachment to parents. The results were mixed: some studies show no significant difference, while others show significant impairments among the second generation.

There was one area, however, in which every single study of the many that I have examined, namely Barocas and Barocas (1980); Brom, Kfir and Dasberg (1994); Danieli (1981); Gross (1988); Guy (1995); Hadar (1988); Karr (1973); Klein (1971); Mazor and Tal (1966); Shefet (1994); Solkoff (1981); Solomon, Kotler and Mikulincer (1988), and Zwerling (1982), arrived at exactly the same finding: the second generation group differed significantly from controls by being more attached to their parents and less able adequately to negotiate the process of *separation–individuation*.

I am using the term "separation–individuation" in the way Mahler (1968) defines it: the process by which both mother and baby gradually emerge from their initial "oneness", and the transformation of their relationship from *immersion* to *relatedness*. During this process, the baby becomes aware of his own Self as distinct and separate from that of the mother.

It appears that this process of emerging from immersion into relatedness is universally impaired in Holocaust survivors' families.

These findings have three important implications.

The first is that people who are born to Holocaust survivors do form a distinct group, with a specific common denominator. The second is that the common denominator is some sort of an attachment disturbance, which does not allow the second generation to separate and "be themselves". The third is that, because parents and children in these families remain in a state of "oneness", to a large degree any disturbance in the parents could be directly experienced by their children, who have not completely separated. As Bergmann has put it:

> The Holocaust trauma is probably transmitted with devastating effect to the child precisely because the parents could not assist in the process of separation. (1982, p. 265)

Now let me change the angle of our exploration, and look at the question of trauma transmission from the perspective of the parents, the survivors of massive trauma.

Massive trauma

It is impossible and meaningless to measure trauma against trauma. It is impossible to compare suffering with suffering. How can one total anguish be any larger or smaller than another? Yet the expression "massive trauma" assumes some yardstick, which renders some kinds of trauma bigger, more devastating than others. I suggest that the best yardstick for the enormity of the trauma lies in our own incapacity to bear witness to it; or in the level of dissociation that listening to it inflicts on the witnesses.

Normally, we understand someone else's pain through our own feelings of empathy: "How would I feel if I found that I had cancer, or if my partner had died?" We flinch when we see a violent scene on television because we imagine it happening to ourselves; we cry with the bereaved, because we are able to imagine our own loved ones taken from us; and, sometimes, we "can't watch" certain things, when they surpass the limit of our capacity or willingness for empathy. To my mind, the differentiating factor between what is called "massive trauma" and any other traumatic experience, is that the former is beyond the limit of *anyone's* ability or willingness to feel empathy for, or to be "able to watch": anyone, including the victims themselves. This leaves the survivors utterly alone, as well as injured. As Freud wrote in *Civilization and Its Discontents* (1930a): "We may shrink in terror at the thought of certain situations: that of the galley-slaves in antiquity ... [or] of the Jews awaiting a pogrom. *It is impossible for us to feel ourselves into the position of these people"* (p. 89, italics mine).

Forty years after these words and a Holocaust later, Niederland (1968), having interviewed hundreds of concentration camp survivors, states:

> In examining a great many survivors of Nazi persecution I have again and again become aware of our consistent incapacity to imagine, much less to evaluate, the nature of the experience. (p. 61)

The "incapacity" that Niederland talks about seems to affect anyone who comes into contact with survivors, including the most empathic health professionals.

In one of his many examples of this phenomenon, Niederland describes a meticulous twelve page hospital report about a Holocaust survivor patient, complete with:

> ... all the details about his childhood illnesses, the condition of his grandfather, grandmother, and the patient's early and later masturbation; but, about his five years in Auschwitz ... [remaining] the only survivor of a family of 91 people, there is one line—*I repeat, one line* ... specifically, the one line says, "This man was in Auschwitz for five years". (ibid., p. 61, italics sic)

This patient had witnessed "... his brothers, sisters transformed into lumps of flesh and blood. One of his children was lying before him, transformed into such a lump" (ibid.). Yet the hospital report neglected even to mention these events. Niederland attributes this neglect to what he calls "the incapacity to imagine" such experiences; an incapacity that induces a sort of blindness, denial, rejection, or simply disbelief, in people coming in contact with survivors of massive trauma. In today's language, we could say that such trauma evokes dissociation in the countertransference.

Dissociation

Most of my work at present is with severely traumatised people who have dissociative disorders. People who, from early infancy, suffered prolonged neglect, cruelty, and often the most unimaginable forms of sadistic abuse, usually at the hands of their attachment figure. And because they were only children or even babies, they were utterly helpless.

Utter helplessness is a key element in the devastating results of trauma. Krystal (1968) calls it "surrender to inevitable danger" (p. 113). Herman (1992) adds that the likelihood of damage increases through "exposure to extreme violence or witnessing grotesque death ... the salient characteristic ... is its power to inspire helplessness and terror" (p. 34). Niederland details the damaging elements:

> 1. The constant pervasive threats and reality of torture and death. 2. Extreme deprivation and suffering. 3. The necessity

of ... suppression of any aggressive or altruistic reaction. 4. The immersion in death in its most ghastly and grotesque forms as a ... factor of daily experience. 5. A permanent psychological mark—*death imprint*—in subjects exposed to such massive traumatization. (Krystal & Niederland, 1971, p. 7)

Our inability fully to engage with accounts of massive trauma can only be matched by the inability of the victims themselves. Indeed, the distance that we experience in attempting to listen to accounts of massive trauma is a reflection of the same psychic process which occurs in the person who is subjected to such traumatic experience.

In the most devastating or terrifying moments, when deadly claws are about to sink into one's body, or into a loved one, with nothing that could stop them, all thoughts stop. The basic world of instincts takes over. Those who can, fight. Those who cannot fight, try flight. And the ones who are helplessly trapped, unable to fight or escape, freeze. What appears from the outside to be a freeze reaction or numb compliance is, in fact, dissociation. We might say that dissociation is a sort of extraordinary flight reaction: when a person can do nothing to save themselves or their loved ones, when both fight and flight are impossible, the mind, or parts of it, splits off from the body, and escapes without it. The body, with any parts of the self that could not escape, remains in place to take the inevitable; but parts of one's self remain "safe" by "disowning" any connection to the trauma, as if the terrible thing had not happened, or had not happened to "me". Like the little girl whom John Southgate (1996) talked about many years ago, here at the Bowlby conference, the little girl who explained her drawing to him: "This is me sitting in the ceiling, watching Daddy hurting little girl".

But massive trauma never passes without consequences, and it is only "as if" one can remain unscathed. The little girl who was sexually abused by her father did not remain safely in the ceiling. She was scarred for life. And what I call "scars" is but a euphemism for years and years of dysfunctional life and crippling suffering. As Bettelheim (1990) states: "Despite all outer appearances to the contrary, it is not possible for these victims of past events to have normal lives in the present" (p. 214).

Moreover, the dissociation itself, while being a rather ingenious way to flee the unbearable while it was happening, has debilitating effects on the person's life later on.

Studying survivors' families, I have interviewed a number of survivors and their children. One of my interviewees, Mrs. A., was twelve years old at the beginning of the war, and was on the run and in hiding for five years. When she started talking, it took me a long while to realise the gruesomeness of the events that she was describing. In a perfectly unaffected voice and with an almost expressionless face she related, in precise order, the names of towns she had fled; exact dates; method of transport; the names of participants in each escape attempt; the death toll; methods of executions; the cost of food. In the same unaffected voice she reported the names of people she never saw again, including her father and her mother. Her most terrifying and hopeless moments were made to sound so boring that I had to struggle to maintain my concentration. "It seems totally unreal, you know", she said, after talking, monotonously and without a break, for over an hour. "It is really like the life of someone else; like it happened on another planet".

Clearly, both Mrs. A. and I were quite dissociated from the content of what she was talking about. It was striking how the facts were perfectly remembered by her (unlike repressed material, which is forgotten), but as if they were "someone else's life". And while she was talking, I was able to take detailed notes of these facts, but felt terribly bored. Like her, I, too, was disconnected from what these facts meant.

But while the witnesses (such as myself) can all "turn their gaze away" or dissociate from the horrors, the victims can only do so at a great cost: whole parts of themselves, which are burning in pain and terror, become out of reach. They do not get help; they never get better; they cannot be soothed and they never find out that the war is over. Their tormented existence continues, as Mrs. A. said, "as if on another planet". Only occasionally the horrors become visible: through nightmares, flashbacks, chronic illness, depression and, as we will see later, through their children.

But, for the moment, let us stay with the survivors, and continue to explore the long-term costs of surviving massive trauma.

Identification with the aggressor

In 1933 Ferenczi stated that the predominant defence available to children who are helpless in the hands of abusing adults is *identification with the aggressor*. This defence mechanism is achieved through introjecting the qualities of the aggressor into oneself.

We know that violence and abuse have the most devastating effects when inflicted in childhood or babyhood, particularly if inflicted by the attachment figure. It is generally agreed that the same events would have less damaging consequences if they were inflicted by strangers, or experienced at a later age. This may seem intuitively obvious, but the reason for it is important: while adults may be affected by people, children internalise or *introject* them, as part of normal child development. This is particularly so regarding their attachment figure.

In normal circumstances, introjecting the qualities of the attachment figure helps the child to become independent, caring, and able to look after him—or herself, as the attachment figure had done previously. But if the qualities of the attachment figure are not protective, but are violent, sadistic, and murderous, a child would introject them just the same, and even more so: when the attachment figure is terrifying, introjecting it also serves as a *defence mechanism* against its frightening qualities. Anna Freud demonstrated this well when she quoted a girl who explained to her little brother, who was frightened of dogs: "If you be a doggie, the dog won't bite you" (Sandler & A. Freud, 1985).

Adults, by contrast, are generally less affected by extreme events compared to children, because their identity is already formed. That is to say, they experience events, bad or good, as external to themselves, rather than introjecting them.

However, "In massive psychic trauma, the ego regresses, and we find that childhood susceptibility to trauma returns" (Krystal, 1968, p. 26). This is a very important assertion, as it explains how even adults can be transformed, not just affected, by massive trauma: under sufficient terror, adults, too, can return to a childlike state where new introjects can occur. It is a stark reminder that there are no hard borders between a child and an adult, a victim, an aggressor, or a saint. We are all susceptible. We can all be harmed.

I would like to elaborate on this point, as in my view it is critically important.

Infanticidal attachment

If we consider that the attachment figure is the person who, so to speak, holds the key to safety and survival—such as a mother to a newborn—we can see that in an extreme, relationship based trauma, the people who have the power to inflict or stop the torture can become new, horrendous attachment figures. And with a new attachment figure comes a new attachment behaviour, one that will keep the person safe at the side of the attachment figure. This behaviour may mimic that of the aggressor, identifying with him, or aim to appease the aggressor by being compliant with his or her wishes. (It is worth noting that some forms of mental illness, in particular schizophrenia, may also be seen as a mixture of these reactions to trauma (Kahr, 2007; Ross, 2007).

The traumatic damage that occurs in massive trauma is, thus, damage to the attachment system of the victim, whether a child or an adult. That is so because, in extreme terror, attachment needs are at their most extreme, and therefore they are re-exposed to remoulding, and to being damaged.

The process of traumatisation is thus manifold, and a vicious cycle: extreme terror elicits extreme neediness which brings, in turn, attachment behaviour, aimed at bringing the frightened person closer to the attachment figure and creating a feeling of safety. When the attachment figure does not rescue the victim, and no relief can be found, the victim eventually falls into one of the three defence types that have been described here, or some mixture of them. He or she may *dissociate* from the real situation into an imaginary safety, like John Southgate's little girl in the ceiling. Or, like Anna Freud's little boy who "becomes" the frightening dog, the victim *introjects the perpetrator*. The third way is to *appease* the perpetrator, striving to do what the perpetrator wants: be almost dead, dead, tortured. In the first case, the survivor loses the integrity of the self, by profound splitting. In the two latter cases, new, deadly introjects form a new sense of identity, and new images of safety: the comforting image of the aggressor, or the comforting image of being dead. Niederland called this "a permanent psychological mark— *a death imprint*—in subjects exposed to such massive traumatisation" (1968, p. 7).

While introjecting qualities of the perpetrator reduces the terror, it has a cost, too. Survivors are left with a strong sense of having been contaminated by evil. The feeling of contamination causes additional suffering, in the form of survivors' guilt, depression, and chronic illness.

For some survivors, however, the sense of contamination and the sense of a broken, dissociative self have brought about what seemed to be the complete opposite. Their lives became a constant, frantic attempt at creating a brand new, "clean" life, full of new, intense attachments. For many of them, the deepest way of finding a new life was by producing new life, by having children.

The second generation child: a new attachment figure

For the survivors, having children was like magic. It was a completely new, non-malevolent attachment; it was a proof that, despite all the evil that they had been through, they were whole, and able to produce life; it carried the hope (or illusion?) that new life can replace the dead.

Most Holocaust survivors were, therefore, extremely dedicated and caring parents. Their babies were felt to be their cure, their hope, their lifesavers. Yet the effects of trauma did not disappear in the light of the new life. Encapsulated and dissociated, the trauma remained uncured, unchanged, untouched. And what is more, it was passed on to the next generation, through the natural door of the attachment system.

While most of these parents would have given their lives away to protect their offspring, they could not protect them from the messages of their traumatic introjects, and from the death threats that were carried and implied by them: "There is murder and terror and grief carried inside myself, forever ready to burst, and any sharp move that you make, may cause the bursting". "If I burst, you'll be contaminated too". "You are contaminated already, because you are mine" (Sachs, 1997, p. 36.)

The survivors of the Holocaust continued to carry the terrifying introjects of the perpetrators and their murderous wishes, in a dissociated way. And they needed their children for their healing, for their psychological survival.

The children, naturally depending on their parents (their attachment figures) for their own survival, had to develop attachment behaviour that would ensure they kept the parents alive, and the perpetrator inside the parents mollified. These children had to be always at the ready to soothe, to imitate the aggressor, to comply, to distract, or simply to duck whenever the aggressor appeared. Breaking away from the parents meant denying the parents their attachment figure, thus threatening their lives. As the child's main purpose in life was to heal the parents, failing to do that meant the child had no right to life. A member of a second generation therapy group expressed this very poignantly:

> ... "For years, I was a china doll. Always nice, neat, pretty, well dressed and well-tended. Eating what she is given. Not loving, not angry, not feeling ..." *The doll belonged to her [her mother], and she*

held on to it with both hands. So everyone knew that I was hers and
she wasn't alone. (Wardi, 1992, p. 75)

That feeling, that "the doll is for mother" is the ultimate expression of
individuation impairment. It says that the child is not even fully alive
in the present, because it is only mother's doll; and that a form of killing
has, already, taken place.

The second generation children did not have the safety which is
needed for *individuation*. They had to stay very closely observant of
their parents' smallest mood changes and needs, and fit in with those in
the best way, for the sake of survival. This is disorganised attachment.

Furthermore, these children had to rely on the love of an attachment
figure who had a murderous aggressor internalised. This is *infanticidal
(disorganised) attachment* (Kahr, 2007; Sachs, 2007, 2008, 2010).

At the start of this chapter, I questioned the notion of "trauma transmission". I have asked whether the signs of trauma in the second generation were the actual parental trauma being somehow "transmitted",
and noted that the parents could not possibly reproduce any of their
Holocaust experiences. Furthermore, these parents were, on the whole,
very caring and non-abusive towards their children. It was therefore
hard to see how any trauma could be passed on to their children, or what
could be the substance that might have affected the second generation.

I now suggest that the traumatic substance that was "transmitted"
to the second generation was the dissociated, deadly introjects of
their parents. The dissociative traits and the terrifying introjects constituted permanent changes to survivors' attachment systems, which
were partly rebuilt around the survivors' abusers. For the survivors'
offspring, these were now the qualities of their own attachment figure,
which were invariably damaging. Without any abusive behaviour. And
despite all love.

I would like to demonstrate some of these dynamics through the
following case.

Ruben

Ruben is fifty-four years old, and was born in London. Both his parents
have blue numbers on their arms: Auschwitz survivors. His mother
had had a child "there", a boy who did not survive. His father was
previously married, but Ruben is not sure if he had children. He was

not called by his dead brother's name, but the meaning of his name is "behold, a son", which he thinks is in memory of that child. His mother had had several miscarriages before he was born. She is very small and frail, and has a crooked back. His father is also very thin. When Ruben was a child, they owned a small toyshop: he remembers them "going to work, hand in hand, like Hansel and Gretel—two little children going to fairyland". He knows nothing of their experiences "there", except that there was hunger, and that they both lost all of their families.

Ruben is a wild, fun, larger-than-life character. He is a star chef in a famous restaurant, with hundreds of people who call him their friend. He is also obese, a heavy smoker, a reckless driver, and he never goes to sleep before the small hours, or before he has had lots of alcohol in good company.

His earliest memory is of sitting in front of the table, with a plate of "disgusting, old, cold food" in front of him, and his mother sighing, "Eat, eat, you must be strong and big". He also remembers coming home from school, his tiny parents ready to leave for "Fairyland" (his name for the toyshop), giving him last orders: "The pots are on the stove. Eat everything. Everything". And he ate—with disgust and anger, yet unable to refuse them. "It kills her when you don't eat her food. And she is a terrible cook. I sometimes think she does it deliberately, to teach us not to be spoiled—we may not survive the next famine if we were!"

Despite the joking manner in which he speaks of his parents' "fear of the next famine", he himself grossly overeats. The obvious thought is that he has introjected his parents' fears of starvation, and eats to protect himself against such risk; but there is more to it.

His frequent referral to his parents as "Hansel and Gretel" suggests a rather sinister association to food. The two children were chased away from their home by an evil stepmother only to fall into the more evil hands of the witch in the candy house, who kept them in a cage and fed them in order for them to grow fat enough so that she could cook and eat them.

Food, in Ruben's experience, was not an expression of parental love and care, nor was it nice. It was "cold, old and disgusting", and he had to eat it because, "It kills her if you don't eat".

He calls his parents Hansel and Gretel because he sees them as vulnerable and childlike, and they were nearly "cooked in the oven", in Auschwitz.

But Ruben, too, was a frightened child in the forest, with only these frightened little "Hansel and Gretel" parents to protect him—that is, if they could. If you recall, he had had a brother, who was killed, unprotected by his mother. His attachment behaviour, therefore, had to ensure that his mother was alive, and strong enough to be able to come to his rescue. The most obvious power that he had in order to achieve these aims was to eat. And his excessive eating may now be understood as a frantic, desperate attachment behaviour.

But he has other sides to him, too: the reckless driving, the heavy smoking, the wild lifestyle. It may look quite surprising that, being so concerned about his parents' fears, he nevertheless lives so dangerously, which, he says, worries them terribly. Is he expressing some sense of independence, rebelliousness, individuation or "true self" after all? Having interviewed his father, I tend to think not.

The way Ruben's father spoke about his big, well-fed, and fearless son, so different from the fragile, sickly parents, was almost smug. And I could almost hear a sound of admiration and pride in his complaints about Ruben's careless behaviour.

Furthermore, the constant fear for Ruben's life allowed his parents to talk about their grief and preoccupation with the death of a son, and thus to express their pain, otherwise mute, about Ruben's dead brother.

Shefet (1994) had called the second generation's attempts to make their parents happy "the impossible task" (p. 23). To elaborate on this, I would say that, in order to help their parents survive, these children had to fulfil many tasks and avoid many pitfalls. They had to become experts at making their parents happy, and at letting their parents grieve; at being very "alive", and at being like a dead person; at being one with the parents, being different from them, being very successful, depressed, ill, and in danger, and, most important, being all of that forever.

We can see Ruben frantically attempting all these tasks. In the words of Suttie and Suttie (1932), "The helpless infant would do everything within its powers to preserve itself, i.e. to maintain its close association with the mother" (p. 209). Whatever that might take.

Summary

Survivors of massive trauma, of all ages, have dissociated, deadly introjects, which either represent (in children) or replace (in adults) parts of their original attachment figures. In other words, as a result of their trauma they develop an *infanticidal attachment* pattern. These introjects are subsequently expressed towards their own children, and are perceived as death threats. Introjects and expressions vary, according to the specific trauma that the survivor has undergone, but they are always deadly, as they were modelled in the image of a murderous perpetrator.

The children, subsequently, dedicate their lives to appeasing the aggressor, whom they cannot escape, as the aggressor lives in the same body as their attachment figure. They develop what Winnicott (1960) called a "false self", a self which is whatever the parents need them to be, a "doll"; and their individuation becomes severely impaired. A vicious cycle is set in motion, as the impairment in individuation exposes the children even more to the parental introjects and death threats, and the attachment of the second generation becomes disorganised, or, often, infanticidal.

Tragically, the damage of atrocities goes far beyond the duration of the traumatic experience. Because what gets damaged is the attachment system of the survivors, it continues to affect their children, generation after generation.

I would like to end with a brief word about healing, which is the ultimate aim of all our attempts to understand.

In 2007, four creative clinicians (Becker, T., Karriker, W., Overkamp, B. & Rutz, C. 2008) conducted a major survey on extreme abuse, in which they explored the views of some 2,000 survivors on various questions, including the relative helpfulness of fifty-two healing methods. The results of the survey show that the three healing methods which were marked "great help" most frequently were individual psychotherapy, personal prayer, and supportive friends. From an attachment perspective, it is notable that all three involve closeness, and someone listening. It is as though what helps to heal the damage of a murderous attachment is a new, benign, and deep relatedness.

If we cannot stop atrocities from happening in the first place, may we be willing to listen to the survivors. Through our ability to hear evil, we may enable its victims to draw on the resource of our shared humanity.

References

Anon. (1985). Poem by a second-generation Holocaust survivor. In: A. Sachs (1997), *Invisible Violence: On the Mechanism of Intergenerational Transmission of Massive Trauma* [unpublished dissertation, City University, London].

Barocas, A. & Barocas, B. (1980). Separation individuation conflicts in children of Holocaust survivors. *Journal of Contemporary Psychotherapy*, *11*(1): 6–14.

Becker, T., Karriker, W., Overkamp, B. & Rutz, C. (2008). The extreme abuse surveys: Preliminary findings regarding dissociative identity disorder. In: A. Sachs & G. Galton (Eds.), *Forensic Aspects of Dissociative Identity Disorder*. London: Karnac.

Bergmann, M. S. (1982). Thoughts on superego pathology of survivors and their children. In: M. S. Bergmann & M. Jucovy (Eds.), *Generations of the Holocaust*. New York: Columbia University Press, 1990.

Bettelheim, B. (1990). Children of the Holocaust. In: B. Bettelheim, *Recollections and Reflections* (p. 214). London: Thames & Hudson.

Brom, D., Kfir, R. & Dasberg, H. (1994). A controlled double-blind study on the offspring of Holocaust survivors. [Paper presented at the 10th annual conference of the International Society for Traumatic Stress Studies, Chicago.] In: Guy, H. (1995), Happiness, intimacy and sexual satisfaction in children of Holocaust survivors. [Unpublished dissertation, Tel Aviv University. Paper presented at the International Congress on Trauma, Jerusalem, 1996.]

Danieli, Y. (1981). Differing adaptation styles in families of survivors of the Nazi Holocaust. *Children Today*, *10*: 6–10.

Ferenczi, S. & Dupont, J. (Eds.) (1933). *The Clinical Diary of Sandor Ferenczi*. Cambridge, MA: Harvard University Press, 1988.

Freud, S. (1930a). *Civilization and Its Discontents*. S. E., *21*: pp. 64–145. London: Hogarth & the Institute of Psychoanalysis.

Gross, S. (1988). The relationship of severity of the Holocaust condition to survivors' child-rearing abilities and their offspring's mental health. *Family Therapy*, *15*(3): 211–221.

Guy, H. (1995). Happiness, intimacy and sexual satisfaction in children of Holocaust survivors. [Unpublished dissertation, Tel Aviv University. Paper presented at the International Congress on Trauma, Jerusalem, 1996.]

Hadar, I. (1988). Second Generation to the Holocaust. Paper presented in Amcha Congress, Jerusalem. Cited in Guy, H. (1995), Happiness, intimacy and sexual satisfaction in children of Holocaust survivors. [Unpublished dissertation, Tel Aviv University. Paper presented at the International Congress on Trauma, Jerusalem, 1996.]

Herman, J. (1992). *Trauma and Recovery*. New York: Basic.

Kahr, B. (2007). Infanticidal attachment. *Attachment: New Directions in Psychotherapy and Relational Psychoanalysis*, *1*: 117–132.

Karr, S. (1973). Second generation effects of the Nazi Holocaust. *Dissertation Abstracts International*, *34*(6): 2935–2936.

Klein, H. (1971). Families of Holocaust survivors in the kibbutz: Psychological studies. In: H. Krystal & W. Niederland (Eds.), *Psychic Traumatization*. Boston: Little, Brown.

Kogan, I. (1995). *The Cry of Mute Children*. London: Free Association.

Krystal, H. (Ed.) (1968). *Massive Psychic Trauma*. New York: International Universities Press.

Krystal, H. & Niederland, W. (Eds.) (1971). *Psychic Traumatization*. Boston: Little, Brown.

Mahler, M. (1968). *On Human Symbiosis and the Vicissitudes of Individuation, Vol. 1*. New York: International Universities Press.

Mazor, A. & Tal, I. (1966). Intergenerational transmission: The individuation process and the capacity for intimacy of adult children of Holocaust survivors. *Contemporary Family Therapy, 18*(1): 95–113.

Niederland, W. (1968). An interpretation of the psychological stresses and defenses in concentration-camp life and the late after-effects. In: H. Krystal (Ed.), *Massive Psychic Trauma*. New York: International Universities Press.

Ross, C. A. (2007). *The Trauma Model: A Solution to the Problem of Comorbidity in Psychiatry*. Richardson, TX: Manitou Communications.

Sachs, A. (1997). Invisible violence: On the mechanism of intergenerational transmission of massive trauma. [Unpublished dissertation, City University, London.]

Sachs, A. (2007). Infanticidal attachment: Symbolic and concrete. *Attachment: New Directions in Psychotherapy and Relational Psychoanalysis, 1*: 297–304.

Sachs, A. (2008). Infanticidal attachment: the link between dissociative identity disorder and crime. In: A. Sachs & G. Galton (Eds.), *Forensic Aspects of Dissociative Identity Disorder*. London: Karnac.

Sachs, A. (2010). As thick as thieves: The ritual abuse family—an attachment perspective on a forensic relationship. In: V. Sinason (Ed.), *Attachment, Trauma and Multiplicity*. Hove: Brunner-Routledge.

Sachs, A. & Galton, G. (Eds.) (2008). *Forensic Aspects of Dissociative Identity Disorder*. London: Karnac.

Sandler, J. & Freud, A. (1985). *The Analysis of Defense: The Ego and the Mechanisms of Defense Revisited*. New York: International Universities Press.

Shefet, R. (1994). Filial commitment as an impossible task in the children of Holocaust survivors. *Sihot-Dialog, 9*(1): 23–27.

Sinason, V. (Ed.) (2002). *Attachment, Trauma and Multiplicity*. Hove, UK: Brunner-Routledge.

Solkoff, N. (1981). Children of survivors of the Nazi Holocaust: A critical review of the literature. *American Journal of Orthopsychiatry, 51*(1): 29–142.

Solomon, Z., Kotler, M. & Mikulincer, M. (1988). Combat-related post-traumatic stress disorder among second generation of Holocaust survivors: Transgenerational effects among Israeli soldiers. *American Journal of Psychiatry, 145*(7): 865–868.

Southgate, J. (1996). An attachment perspective on dissociation and multiplicity. [A paper presented at the Third Annual John Bowlby Memorial Lecture, The Bowlby Centre, London.]

Suttie, I. & Suttie, J. (1932). The mother: Agent or object? *British Journal of Medical Psychology, 12*: 199–233.

Wardi, D. (1992). *Memorial Candles: Children of the Holocaust*. London: Routledge.

Winnicott, D. W. (1960). Ego distortion in terms of true and false self. In: *The Maturational Process and the Facilitating Environment*. New York: International Universities Press.

Zwerling, I. (1982). A comparison of parent–child attachment and separation in American and Holocaust survivor families. [Paper presented at AMHAI meeting, Chicago.] In: Wardi, D. (1992), *Memorial Candles: Children of the Holocaust*. London: Routledge.

CHAPTER FOUR

The place of fear in attachment theory and psychoanalysis: the fifteenth John Bowlby Memorial Lecture

Arietta Slade

Introduction

Today I will be talking about fear and its place in attachment theory and psychoanalysis. In the hierarchy of human motivations, Bowlby placed particular emphasis on attachment because it is essential to our physical and psychological survival. And he privileged fear of loss and danger because these elemental reactions drive and organise the activation and deactivation of the attachment system, regulate physical and psychological proximity seeking and contact maintenance, and shape the organisation of mental life.

At the time that Bowlby began formulating his theory of human attachment, psychoanalysis placed virtually no emphasis on the role of fear and the search for safety in the development of personality and psychopathology. This had much to do, of course, with Freud's particular interest in internal reality, and his relative lack of interest in relationships. Bowlby, by contrast, was greatly interested in actual experience, and believed that attending to the dynamics of fear and its regulation within the context of actual attachment relationships would fundamentally change psychoanalysis (1969, 1973, 1980, 1988). For Bowlby, an emphasis on fear and the search for safety offered a crucial corrective to the theories of motivation, development, and psychopathology that prevailed in psychoanalysis at the time. For many years, however, this corrective fell on deaf ears within the analytic community, which actively rejected Bowlby and his ideas for several decades.

Things began to change dramatically in the early 1990s, however, when—thanks largely to the extraordinary work of Mary Ainsworth (Ainsworth, Blehar, Waters & Wall, 1978) and Mary Main (Main, 2000; Main, Kaplan & Cassidy, 1985)—contemporary psychoanalysis began to embrace the term "attachment" and to make it a central part of its lexicon. But as I hope to make clear today, I believe that—as much as psychoanalysis has become a relational theory—Bowlby's (as well as Ainsworth's and Main's) crucial emphasis on fear and its regulation remains largely unappreciated, even today. That is, as much as most clinicians—and especially those who work with traumatised patients—work with fear all the time, what is in fact a crucial paradigm shift has yet to substantially affect psychoanalytic and clinical theory. This despite the fact that speaking to the dynamics of fear and the search for safety provide us with direct, experience near ways of engaging many of our patients and understanding the particular nature of their internal worlds. And it provides them and us with a way of understanding not only how we come to be who we are, but why.

As I hope to make clear today, incorporating an attachment perspective into both theory and clinical practice goes well beyond acknowledging the centrality of early attachment relationships in the formation of character. To truly reflect the essential aspects of Bowlby's theory, and particularly his emphasis on the evolutionary value of both fear and attachment, contemporary psychoanalysis must address the dynamics of fear and its regulation, in development as well as in the clinical situation.

Thus, in line with the theme of this book, I will be writing about fear and its place in psychoanalysis. Or better put, I will be describing the ways that the relative lack of attention to the *driving, organising force of fear and the search for safety* has been problematic for psychoanalysis, and—by extension—for clinical practice. I will begin, of course, with Bowlby, and his views on the place of fear in human experience, and link this to the mother–infant relationship. I will then consider some of the reasons for the relative neglect of fear within psychoanalysis. Finally, I will discuss some of the clinical implications of assigning fear and the search for safety the primacy they so rightly deserve in both clinical theory and practice.

Bowlby and the paradigm shift for psychoanalysis

Beginning in the 1950s, John Bowlby described the human animal in a way that was fundamentally different from prevailing, notably Freudian, views of human nature. Bowlby's thinking was rooted in biology and profoundly Darwinian, and revolved around the notion that we—like all species—are biologically programmed to enhance our chances of survival, and thus preserve the species, at all costs. His theory emphasised our biological heritage, and in this our essential tie to other animal species.

Like Freud, Bowlby believed that as human beings we share a number of essential features with each other. Also like Freud, he understood that the feature that is most essential to man as opposed to other higher mammals is the development of an elaborated mental life. But what distinguished Bowlby's work most dramatically from that of his psychoanalytic forebears, and even contemporaries, was his "commitment to applying the scientific method to a field steeped in dogma" (Richard Bowlby, personal communication, March 7, 2008). And for Bowlby, the science of evolution and Darwin's emphasis on survival most directly contradicted what he viewed as the dogma of classical psychoanalysis. For Bowlby, the drive to survive—not just physically, but psychologically—was key to understanding the organisation of mental life. To couch this in more contemporary terms—our biology, core elements of our neural make-up, our arousal systems, our cognitive apparati, our representations of self and other are organised, at least in part, by our instinct to survive. We survive by forming relationships, and adapting to the minds of others. Relationships are the remedy for fear—of loss, of annihilation, of psychic emptiness—and offer us the deepest expression of our humanity.

The fear system is evolutionarily selected because it is crucial to our safety, and to the activation and deactivation of the attachment system. Fear for his survival is what sends the child back to the safety of his caregiver, and regulates physical and psychological proximity. It also modifies his natural exploration of the world around him. Autonomous exploration is as crucial to our survival as is attachment, and indeed a healthy attachment relationship grounds exploration in a feeling of safety, authenticity, and freedom. Unregulated or dysregulated fear, however, can distort exploration, and with it the development of a mental life.

I want to make clear that I am not just referring to extreme fear or trauma. The fear system is always primed, for crucial evolutionary reasons, and so some part of our brains is always "keeping an eye out". Fear and anxiety are part—hopefully a small part—of everyday life. When we feel threatened, our attachment system is activated, and when we achieve safety (via proximity), the attachment system is deactivated. However, it is uncontained or unregulated fear that leads to psychopathology and maladaptation. The secure child experiences fear within the context of knowing that his caregiver will provide comfort and safety. He knows that she will lessen his anxiety, quiet his fears, and help him feel safe and ready for his next adventure. But when the awareness of danger, most perniciously from the caregiver herself, persists even at low levels, the fear system is chronically elevated and dysregulated, and begins to infiltrate the child's experience, his sense of the other, his sense of his own body, and his sense of his autonomy. Higher levels of fear more directly inhibit exploration. In any event, regardless of the level of fear, the child is tied to the caregiver, because she is essential to his survival, even if she is threatening his very being.

To reiterate, I want to emphasise that for fear to serve its signal function, it must be kept at manageable levels, and regulated by the attachment figure. When fear is regulated within the context of the attachment relationship, exploration is satisfying and rich, and a full appreciation of the other is possible. When chronic fear, even at relatively low levels, is unmodulated, exploration and self-discovery are distorted, and the child feels helpless, angry, and more frightened. At the extreme, as described by Fonagy (Fonagy, Gergely, Jurist & Target, 2002), he feels unreal and alien, even to himself. It is these distortions that are reflected in the typologies of insecure attachment.

Bowlby suggested that we are left with a few basic ways of adapting to our fear of losing the other, and thus our self. The "patterns of attachment" that he sketched out in his writings—and that were later elaborated by Mary Ainsworth and even more fully, Mary Main—were simple and straightforward. These patterns were conceived as "rational" adaptations to the competing demands of survival and self-expression. The child who feels safe in knowing that his needs will be met is *secure*, while the child or adult who is in some small or large way frightened for his safety and psychological survival is *insecure*. The avoidant individual chooses thin autonomy over intimacy, the preoccupied individual prefers fraught intimacy over autonomy, and the disorganised or unresolved individual finds safety in neither. These adaptations are finally, ultimately rational within the context of an individual's history in relationships—this is what he or she has had to do to survive.

Importantly, neuroscientists have in recent years focused a great deal of attention on the fear system. Contemporary interpreters of neuroscience such as Allan Schore (2003) and Daniel Siegel (1999) have made it abundantly clear that not only are the attachment and fear systems rooted in our biology, but their regulation affects our biology as well. The functioning of higher cortical systems—thinking, mentalisation, symbolisation, etc.—emerge as a function of the regulation of the sympathetic nervous system and the hypothalamic-pituitary-adrenal axis (HPA). The social environment, namely the relationship, plays a prominent role in such regulation, and in priming the part of the brain that processes emotions. Fear and its vicissitudes, whether at extreme or chronic, lower levels, preclude or distort learning and higher levels of synthetic, integrative functioning. In short, insecure attachments, particularly in their more pathological forms, reflect neural and hormonal adaptations to chronic stress and fear. And the healing power of new, more secure attachments cannot help but lead to changes at both physiological and psychological levels.

Mother and baby

In order to bring some of these concepts alive, I will now briefly describe an interaction between a young mother and her infant daughter. Charmaine was a participant in *Minding the Baby*, an intensive home visiting programme that provides mental health and nursing services to high risk young mothers and their babies, beginning in pregnancy (Slade et al., 2005; Slade, Sadler & Mayes, 2005). Charmaine had her baby at eighteen. She had a long history of trauma, including parental abandonment, foster placement, and sexual abuse. As part of our research, we saw Charmaine and her baby in a standard face-to-face interaction setting when the baby was four months old.

Charmaine was asked to interact with her daughter as she ordinarily would, but without toys or other objects; they were simply to engage with one another *en face*. Charmaine found this instruction very difficult: her baby was just waking up from a nap, she was (we learned later) hungry, and Charmaine felt pressured to "perform" for the camera. What resulted was an alarming interaction in which Charmaine intruded upon Sophia's physical and visual space in an extremely aggressive way for nearly twenty minutes. She poked, she loomed, she slapped in a playful but rough way, and she mocked Sophia's distress. Charmaine smiled throughout, albeit a tight, forced smile, and indicated with her vocal prosody that she was "playing". But the baby's cues that she was distressed, overwhelmed, and frightened were over-ridden, again and again.

The baby looked stunned, and attempted in a variety of ways to regulate her mother's insistent and overwhelming approach. At moments she looked away and seemed almost dissociated, at others she looked actively frightened and blinked her eyes as if trying to blot her mother out, at others she fussed mildly, and at others she struggled to placate with a dazed half smile. Often all of these efforts were taking place at once. What was most striking was that she rarely fully broke gaze with her mother; she could not take the "alone" and integrative time so vital in any *en face* interaction (Brazelton & Cramer, 1990) because she could not risk letting her mother out of her sight. As a result, she had no opportunity to do what is natural and organising in social interaction: to turn away, regulate one's own internal experience and re-engage. Nor did she have the opportunity to shape the interaction, and in so doing to create and play. She was on full alert for what in baby terms is a very long time, and was both physiologically and psychologically highly stressed. There was little safety to be had, only continuing and fluctuating fear.

At four months, this child was stuck in the paradox Main and Hesse (1990) have so beautifully described in their work on the roots of disorganised attachment. She was afraid, but the impulse to seek comfort from the caregiver was thwarted because the caregiver is the *source of fear*. In this instance, what under more benign circumstances would automatically be a signal to the mother to comfort and reas-sure the child became a kind of invitation to continue the frighten-ing interaction. Sophia's fear was unmetabolised and unmentalised by the mother. As Main and Hesse as well as Karlen Lyons-Ruth (Lyons-Ruth & Jacobvitz, 1999) have described, it is this paradox that is at the heart of disorganised attachment: organised strategies such as either withdrawal or clinging are each too dangerous, and a *disorganised* strategy is the result.

Ten months later, after intensive home intervention, Sophia was observed in the Strange Situation. Based upon what we observed at four months, we would have predicted that Sophia would be disorganised in relation to attachment. But she was not. She was visibly upset by the separation, but upon her mother's return greeted her openly, and actively sought proximity and comfort from Charmaine, who picked her up and cuddled her close. Sophia's legs wrapped around her mother's torso, and she snuggled in against her neck, quickly calming down. After comforting Sophia very effectively, Charmaine engaged her in looking at a book. In this instance, intensive intervention activated the mother's capacity to mentalise and to respond sensitively to her baby. The baby was classified as secure at one year; she turned to her mother for comfort and safety when distressed, and her mother provided it, clearly and sensitively.

This is not to say that the coast is clear for this dyad. There are indications in the Strange Situation, but more prominently in the clinical material collected over the course of home visits that anger was a continuing problem in this family and in this child. While treatment activated the mother's feelings of connection and concern for the child, the preferred mode of interacting with her continued to be somewhat intrusive and overstimulating, and the mother's own traumatic history invaded the relationship in a variety of ways. The father had a lengthy history of violence, and only slowly began to be more nurturing and loving in interaction with his adored child. For Sophia, the residue of the anger that must have accumulated at being scared and unheard for so long inevitably found their expression in behaviour. She was prone to tantrums and anger, and favoured a kind of primitive identification with the aggressor. While her anger was not so powerful as to disrupt her attachment security, and was surely modulated by her parents' greatly improved capacity to comfort and nurture her, it did continue to affect her development.

These examples illustrate a fundamentally human situation: feeling threatened, and seeking care from one's caregiver. At four months, the child was faced with the paradox of her caregiver being the source of fear, fear that could not be resolved in the usual way, namely by obtaining comfort from her. At fourteen months, the child was readily able to seek her comfort at a moment of high intensity affect, in this case fear and anger.

Fear and its place in psychoanalysis

For many decades, fear had no real place in psychoanalysis. Anxiety, yes, but in a totally different sense than that emphasised by Bowlby. The failure to recognise the central role of fear and its regulation had largely to do with Freud's early failure to recognise that his patients could feel (and actually be!) threatened or seduced by their caregivers (Freud & Breuer, 1895d). In these earliest days of psychoanalysis, he turned away from fear, fear of *real* danger, fear for one's safety, for one's very existence. In doing so, he failed to appreciate the dimensions and relevance of this essential human experience, the capacity for which is hard-wired in our brains, links us to all other mammalian species, and is essential to our survival. Instead he suggested that fear, or anxiety, emerged when impulses or fantasies threatened the integrity of the ego. While in his later work he linked anxiety to the loss of the mother's love, he for the most part—even after this shift in his thinking—saw the mother or libidinal object's central role as reducing unwanted excitation (Wachtel, 2008). Freud's brilliant vision of *man in conflict* utterly transformed Western thought, and gave rise to crucial insights about what it means to be human. However, his relative failure to emphasise the dynamics of fear and the search for safety as a *central and critical human conflict* was most unfortunate for psychoanalysis. In a number of crucial ways, Freud never fully appreciated that one of our primary aims, as living creatures, is to survive, and as highly evolved mammals, to seek relationships that will ensure our survival, on many levels. In this crucial way, he failed to integrate Darwin's fundamental premise into his thinking. It fell to Bowlby to do this. And even today, relational psychoanalysis lacks a dynamic, motivational theory.

This is not to say that Bowlby saw the "darker" sides of our essential nature as irrelevant to our survival as a species; indeed, he was well aware of their role in evolution, and of their importance in human experience. But he insisted that aggression, rage, sexuality, and the fantasies that accompany such experiences emerge against the backdrop and within the context of the attachment relationship. Aggression and sexuality are crucial to healthy development, to signalling our caregivers when we are dysregulated, to our autonomy, separateness, and pleasure in exploration, and to our ability to find full satisfaction in our bodies and in our relationships. But within the context of disrupted attachment, the potential for distortion of these fundamental elements of our humanity is enormous.

Historical roots

Freud's failure to recognise the centrality of fear had deep personal roots. In fact, one could see this failure—at least in part—as a function of the dynamics of his own attachment organisation. In his compelling biography, *Freud: Darkness in the Midst of Vision*, Louis Breger (2000), argues that Freud's own early experience of trauma and loss deeply shaped the nature of his thinking and thus, the history of psychoanalysis. Before reading this book I had imagined Freud's childhood to have been one of relative and bourgeois comfort and ease, this version of Freud's life having been that widely promulgated by Freud and his biographers (see, for instance, Gay, 1988). Thus, I was very surprised by Breger's detailed description of an early life marked by numerous disruptions and traumas. Freud was the first of eight children born in ten years to his parents, Jacob and Amalia Freud. Jacob married Amalia, twenty years his junior, after having been widowed twice; tragically, he also lost his own father just before his first son, Sigmund, was born. Some eleven months after Sigmund's birth, another boy was born, only to die of an undisclosed illness a short six months later. It is hard to imagine that this was not a household filled with sadness and grief, its impact on Freud profound and pervasive. Anecdotal reports by extended family members suggest that his mother was quite depressed; in addition, the subsequent birth of six more siblings over the next eight years surely made it unlikely that she could remain emotionally available to her oldest child, as much as she treasured and favoured him. In fact, ongoing experiences of relative neglect must have been very confusing and infuriating for a boy who was in so many ways the "chosen one" among his siblings. On top of these very real challenges to his sense of safety and security, his mother periodically required rather long hospital stays for treatment of tuberculosis throughout his childhood. In addition, his beloved nanny was precipitously fired when he was three (Bowlby likewise lost his nanny at an early age).

Poverty was an ongoing fact of life for this family. Until Freud was four, the family lived in a one-room apartment in a small town. His father (along with his mother) ran a wool business, but even in the best of times this was barely enough to keep the family solvent. When Freud was four, his father's business failed altogether, forcing the family to move into the Jewish ghetto in Vienna, closer to their extended family. From this point on, his father was unable to support his family with any consistency whatsoever; the result was a life of chronic poverty, living in extremely crowded conditions, without easy access to many of life's necessities. Freud did not have his own room until he was nineteen. The family was regularly rescued from financial ruin by extended family members, who helped out when times were especially dire. Well into his twenties, and even after his marriage, Freud was financially supported by mentors and benefactors.

Interestingly, this is not the story Freud himself told of his childhood, but these are the facts of his upbringing. Clearly, he was no stranger to trauma and loss, and fear must have been a familiar experience for him, at least at some level, throughout his childhood. Indeed, Breger makes the case that with Freud understandably scarred by his own early traumatic and relational experiences, his theory (and indeed personality) emerged in an attempt to defend against the impact of these early experiences. That is, his inability to metabolise or recognise the force and impact of his early traumas led him to focus on the *sequelae* of disrupted early experience, namely aggression, competitiveness, impulsiveness, destructiveness, and the like. Along these lines, Breger further suggests that many of the very real emotional and relational difficulties Freud struggled with throughout his life can be understood in light of these early disruptions.

Retrospective psychoanalysis is inherently problematic, but if we believe that the past shapes our mental life, how can Freud's early experience not be relevant to his vision of humanity? Freud's story is not so different from those we hear from the high-risk families that we see in our community intervention programmes. And yet Freud all but ignored what must have been the enormous disruptions he experienced in his primary attachment relationships, focusing instead on developments within the later, Oedipal period. But it is impossible to imagine that his Oedipal yearnings were anything but deeply affected by the ongoing experience of fear and anxiety *for his very survival*. It is likely, for instance, that, in the face of his mother's depression, grief, and wish to fill the void opened by the death of her infant, the young Freud experienced both fear of abandonment and the wish to control the uncontrollable. That is, his "infantile neurosis", and particularly his relationships to authority, to sexuality, and to his own aggression, emerged against the backdrop of what was most likely an insecure attachment organisation.

For generations, psychoanalytic historians have described Freud's theory as shaped by the history and culture of the Victorian age. But what struck me so powerfully learning of Freud's early history was how much his theory was shaped by his own personal history, a personal history that has been largely ignored or glossed over in prior biographical accounts. Breger suggests that in a number of ways Freud emphasised the centrality of sexual and aggressive urges in the development of the personality because these aspects of his functioning were enormously compromised and distorted by his attempt to regulate his own fears. Freud certainly struggled greatly with his aggression, as well as with his sexuality. And it seems highly likely that these driving preoccupations were at least in part symptoms of the impact of fear, early loss, deprivation, and trauma on his earliest relationships. I mean neither to be reductionistic, nor to suggest that this is *the* rather than one way to understand some of the personal roots of his theory. But it seems fairly clear that his earliest experiences shaped the history of psychoanalysis in crucial ways, ways that have been largely unappreciated and unrecognised. Bowlby, however, got it.

Fear, safety, and clinical process

When I first learned about attachment theory, I felt as if I was coming home.

While I had actually administered the Strange Situation when I first met Mary Ainsworth in December of 1981, I actually knew little about Bowlby or attachment theory. When I heard Ainsworth talk about the Strange Situation, however, I immediately understood that Ainsworth's (and of course Bowlby's) definition of anxiety was very different from the one I had learned in my training. Listening to her, asking questions, etc., I slowly got it. She was talking about real fear. Insecure babies were afraid of something real; they were afraid that their attachment needs would go unacknowledged and unknown, leaving them vulnerable to psychic threat, potential disorganisation, and annihilation. Maladaptive strategies of maintaining felt security—including anger, , and distorted sexuality—were aimed at warding off this threat and at managing this real fear. What Ainsworth was vividly describing was very different from more psychoanalytic notions of anxiety, anxiety about *internal* experience rather than *external* reality, anxiety about separateness, differentiation, and—more classically—unbridled aggression or libido, rather than about actual abandonment and loss. Everything Ainsworth described also clicked with what had so fascinated me about the new views of infancy offered by Stern, Mahler, and Pine.

When I had the great fortune of attending Mary Main's first Adult Attachment Interview (AAI) training programme four years later, I got it even more clearly. In her categorisation of insecure patterns of language and thought, Main was describing dynamic attempts to regulate fear in the attachment relationship and to establish some, albeit compromised, feeling of safety and connection. The search for safety and the management of fear were manifest in the very structures of thinking and of affect regulation. These ideas were entirely consistent with my clinical work. It seemed natural to me to listen for fear, and to see psychological experience as organised around the fear and anxiety that follow real disruptions, defences against hope, against longing for closeness and connection.

My understanding of fear had a great deal to do with the role fear and the search for safety had played in my own childhood. When I found my way to attachment theory, I realised that the anxiety Ainsworth and Main were talking about was the anxiety I had known. And when I took the AAI, I began to deeply understand how my *actual experience and my coming to grips with fear in my primary relationships* had made me who I was. The fear and anxiety with which I struggled, and that disrupted my relationships now made sense in terms of the repeated abandonments in my earliest months and years. My understanding of *why* was suddenly different, and I began to see these adaptations—troubling as they were—as rational. How else would I have survived? I found in the elegant simplicity of attachment theory a way of understanding how my actual experience and my coming to grips with fear in my primary relationships had made me who I was. It was liberating, for it both changed the way I understood myself, and allowed me to have a new level of compassion for my choices and adaptations. While my experience in analysis up to that point had offered me the solace of deep concern, steady consistency, and the willingness to connect, I now found a way of making sense of what I had experienced in a way that had eluded my first, deeply well-meaning but classically trained analyst, largely because of the tilt of her own training and analytic experience. Ironically, she had herself escaped the Nazis as a young university student and had undoubtedly suffered staggering trauma, fear, and loss in her own life. My second analyst understood my fear in a way that made all the difference.

While my own life experience certainly sensitised me to fear and the search for safety, I want to reiterate what I stated earlier, namely that the experience of fear and the search for safety and comfort in relationships are core *human* experiences. They are not simply the realm of the traumatised. The search for safety is what *drives* us, and what serves as a primary motivation for the formation of our earliest relationships. This was Bowlby's brilliant, transforming, profoundly humane insight: *we ALL do what we must* to maintain our primary relationships because without them we will not survive, physically *or* psychologically. In short, "better safe than dead".

The clinical situation

I want now to deal more specifically with the clinical situation. I want first to suggest that, as much as contemporary psychoanalysis has embraced Bowlby's emphasis on attachment, we have yet to fully appreciate the relevance of his ideas about fear and its evolutionary significance for clinical work.

As an example, so many clinicians use the term attachment and find the notion of attachment classification compelling and clinically relevant. But few, I think, fully appreciate the fact that attachment classifications are not monolithic, impermeable psychic structures. Rather, attachment organisations reflect dynamic efforts to regulate fear and anxiety. And it is these dynamics rather than the categories themselves that deserve our clinical attention. In point of fact, the categories themselves can quite often be fluid in the clinical context. But what is particularly radical about Main's work is the implication that chronic experiences of fear—be they the result of trauma or more subtle distortions of the attachment system—are internalised and transformed in ways that profoundly alter the very organisation of mental life. *Recognising and regulating these fears and their sequelae are the focus of our clinical work.* Understanding, containing, and hopefully transforming the dynamic functioning of the fear system—a system, by the way, that has become a major focus of modern day neuroscience—is at the heart of what we do.

Working within the framework of attachment theory means recognising, feeling, and eventually putting into words the *driving, organising force of fear and the search for safety*. And it means recognising the role of fear and the search for safety in the therapeutic relationship. I think that while we all *understand* these phenomena, we have not fully developed a language for them. Our imagination is limited by old constructs that live on in ways outside of our consciousness.

Paradigms shape our theories and *what we see and hear* in profound ways. Paradigm shifts lead us to see what has always been there in different ways, and to shed light on that which has always been there but has not been fully understood or integrated. An adjustment in our understanding of causality, reversing figure for ground, profoundly changes how we understand the organisation of psychological experience.

The relative failure at a theoretical level to privilege certain types of experiences means that neither we nor our patients can privilege them, either. Privileging fear and the search for safety profoundly changes how we both notice and talk about these experiences with our patients. It also enhances our compassion for our patients and their efforts to survive, compassion that we sorely need when their ways of being in the world and in relation to us are most frustrating, paralysing, and disorganising. In this sense, privileging fear changes the nature of the therapeutic relationship in crucial ways.

In our work with patients, we are trying to recognise and then mentalise the dynamic ways that they regulate fear and the search for safety in their primary relationships. We are trying to imagine the moments in which these dynamic patterns began to take shape—moments of balancing the need for safety with the desire for full autonomy and unfettered connectedness—and we are experiencing these moments in the transference and countertransference, in our brains, in our bodies, and in our minds. Our experience of these dynamic patterns and our imagining their childhood roots allows us to bring them alive in the treatment so the patient can see them, feel them, and *play* with them. The more we appreciate the many ways our patients—like their mammalian forebears—are moving towards and away from the other in their search for security and love, the more we will succeed in finding metaphors and language that capture these core human experiences. Finding dynamic and mutative metaphors is key to the transformation of internal structures, and to helping our patients imagine and then begin to create new and more fulfilling relationships.

As I mentioned earlier, this perspective is entirely consistent with current neuroscience as well as mentalisation theory. Change in psychotherapy does not take place only at the cortical level. In fact, it is likely that changes take place first in the portions of the brain that regulate arousal (i.e., fear), which then pave the way towards higher order change and reorganisation. Many therapists certainly recognise this, and as a result pay close attention to the pre—or non-verbal as well as bodily aspects of the therapeutic relationship (Ogden, Minton & Pain, 2006; Van der Kolk, 2006). In any event, the utility of symbolic language in the clinical setting will depend upon at least some degree of basic physiological regulation and organisation. And it is the therapeutic relationship that is crucial to the development of neural structures that are the bedrock upon which higher order representations emerge.

I would like to close with two brief clinical vignettes, which while insufficient to fully convey what it means to fully respect fear in the clinical situation, are offered as brief illustrations of my thinking.

Barb came to me three years ago, when she discovered that her husband of eighteen years had a secret life with another woman. It quickly became clear that he was deeply entrenched in this other life, and that he would go to great lengths, including extraordinary levels of deception and manipulation, to maintain it. And yet for two years, Barb was again and again seduced by his lies, unable to imagine or believe that she and their children were being so completely cast aside. What was particularly vexing—both to me and often to Barb—was that despite the fact that he was in every way dangerous to her and to their children, she could not reliably maintain any safe distance from him. She would take him back, again and again, wanting to believe that he had either the capacity or the desire to love and care for her. As I said to her when she was berating herself for having—once again—fallen for his lies, "You are so terrified of what's ahead of you that you want to believe he can take care of you. Even though it's as if you and your sons are covered in blood and the knife is in his hand, you can't believe you'll survive on your own". There was silence, then acknowledgment. "No, I really can't".

Barb believed that letting go of her husband—whose own psychopathology was such that he had to obliterate her very emotional core—would lead to her psychic annihilation. My job was to clarify where she was safe and where she was in grave danger. And where she could actually feel safe and free, and where she would surely cease to exist. It was also to redirect her rage, away from herself and towards its actual object: her husband.

Barb was a woman whose fear could easily be missed. She had a tough, no nonsense Midwestern demeanour, and she could be sharp and cutting with her sons and her husband. She could be intensely self-critical. Barb's father was a hateful, bitter, man. He had been terribly wounded in WWII, and lived in chronic, unrelenting pain. He worked the night shift and slept all day, and raged whenever his sleep was disturbed by his family's normal activities. His wife and children lived in terror of his outbursts, their arousal systems perpetually engaged in anticipation of danger. And they lived with his need to derogate and humiliate. For Barb, this was closeness, this was a relationship. The alternative was nothingness; she could not imagine it, her mother could not imagine it, and together the failure of imagination rooted them in terror. It was this dynamic that was repeated again and again in her relationship to her husband.

One way to understand Barb was to see her as identified with the aggressor. But because I saw Barb as dismissing of attachment, and her edgy, flinty, and sometimes harsh demeanour as defensive, as protecting her against fear of her father's rage, of utter solitude, and of her longings for closeness, I did not take on her aggression, per se. I went behind it, to her fear. This is not to say that we did not often talk about why she could be harsh and avoidant; it is to say that we understood this as a manifestation of her fear. As we understood this, she began to be able to acknowledge and express her anger at her husband in appropriate ways, and to establish crucial distance from him. And she became much more affectionate and close to her sons.

A somewhat different example is provided by Cynthia, who came to see me when her relationship with her adolescent daughter became unbearable and unmanageable. Cynthia was referred by her daughter's therapist after he became aware of the pernicious effects of her rage on her child. In my first session with Cynthia, I felt very much the way I imagine the infant I described earlier felt when her mother kept invading her space. While Cynthia was on the surface very proper and agreeable, she flooded me with the story of her own early and deeply scarring childhood, full of abuse, violence, alcohol, and mental illness. She is the sole psychological survivor amongst all her siblings. And yet, this humiliated, abused child had become a humiliating and rageful parent.

Over the course of our work together, Cynthia began to appreciate—in ways that were so reminiscent of Selma Fraiberg's "Ghosts in the Nursery" paper (1980)—that the fear she was eliciting in her daughter was the fear that she herself had known. Her assaults were often triggered by her perception that her daughter was doing something to humiliate her, which justified her being punitive and unyielding. In an effort to override her own feelings of helplessness and fear, she became frightening. When we began our work together, her own fear was dissociated, discovered only through her identification with her daughter's. As the psychic reality of her early experience took hold, and particularly the reality of the degree to which both her parents had assaulted her with words and actions, she began to see her daughter as separate, and frightened. Only then could she protect her child, and have compassion for her own powerful defences and longings.

I would like to conclude by saying that I think that virtually all therapists working today are deeply aware of the pernicious effects of fear and anxiety on their patients' experience of themselves and their relationships. And most, if not all, are well aware of the impact of early attachment experiences on the development of the personality. And yet it is my impression that at this point in time, the essential teachings of contemporary attachment theory, namely that fear and its regulation plays a central role in the organisation of psychic structure, in the organisation of one's sense of self, and in the organisation of the relational world, have yet to be fully understood and incorporated into modern relational psychoanalysis.

Acknowledgements

I am enormously grateful to The Bowlby Centre for Attachment-Based Psychoanalytic Psychotherapy for inviting me to give the John Bowlby Memorial Lecture in the centenary year of his birth. I would especially like to thank Sir Richard and Xenia Bowlby as well as Kate White, Joseph Schwartz, and The Bowlby Centre board, for their generous, kind, and warm welcome. I would also like to thank Jeremy Holmes, Morris Eagle, Karen Gilmore, Fred Pine, Alan and June Sroufe, Jude Cassidy, and Karlen Lyons-Ruth for helping me in my early efforts to articulate these ideas. I also want to thank Lou Breger, whose brilliant book on Freud's own relationship to fear has been an inspiration to me (*Freud: Darkness in the Midst of Vision*, 2000). Finally, I want to thank a dear friend and very smart colleague, who—after hearing me describe the topic of the paper on which this chapter is based—said, "Oh, I get it … better safe than dead!"

References

Ainsworth, M. D. S., Blehar, M. C., Waters, E. & Wall, S. (1978). *Patterns of Attachment: Psychological Study of the Strange Situation*. Hillsdale, NJ: Erlbaum.

Bowlby, J. (1969). *Attachment and Loss: Volume 1. Attachment*. New York: Basic.

Bowlby, J. (1973). *Attachment and Loss: Volume 2. Separation*. New York: Basic.

Bowlby, J. (1980). *Attachment and Loss: Volume 3. Loss*. New York: Basic.

Bowlby, J. (1988). *A Secure Base: Parent–Child Attachment and Healthy Human Development*. New York: Basic.

Brazelton, T. B. & Cramer, B. (1990). *The Earliest Relationship: Parents, Infants and the Drama of Early Attachment*. Reading, MA: Addison-Wesley.

Breger, L. (2000). *Freud: Darkness in the Midst of Vision*. New York: Wiley & Sons.

Fonagy, P., Gergely, G., Jurist, E. & Target, M. (2002). *Affect Regulation, Mentalization, and the Development of the Self*. New York: Other Press.

Fraiberg, S. (Ed.) (1980). *Clinical Studies in Infant Mental Health*. New York: Harper & Row.

Freud, S. & Breuer, J. (1895d). Studies on hysteria. *S. E.*, 2: 1–335. London: Hogarth and the Institute of Psycho-Analysis.

Gay, P. (1988). *Freud: A Life for our Time*. New York: Anchor.

Lyons-Ruth, K. & Jacobvitz, D. (1999). Attachment disorganization: Unresolved loss, relational violence, and lapses in behavioral and attentional strategies. In: J. Cassidy & P. R. Shaver (Eds.), *The Handbook of Attachment Theory and Research* (pp. 520–554). New York: Guilford.

Main, M. (2000). The organised categories of infant, child, and adult attachment. *Journal of the American Psychoanalytic Association, 48*: 1055–1096.

Main, M. & Hesse, E. (1990). Lack of mourning in adulthood and its relationship to infant disorganization: Some speculations regarding causal mechanisms. In: M. Greenberg, D. Cicchetti & M. Cummings (Eds.), *Attachment in the Preschool Years: Theory, Research, and Intervention* (pp. 161–182). Chicago: University of Chicago Press.

Main, M., Kaplan, N. & Cassidy, J. (1985). Security in infancy, childhood and adulthood: A move to the level of representation. *Monographs of the Society for Research in Child Development, Serial, No. 209, 50*: 66–107.

Ogden, P., Minton, K. & Pain, C. (2006). *Trauma and the Body: A Sensorimotor Approach to Psychotherapy*. New York: W. W. Norton.

Schore, A. (2003). *Affect Regulation and the Repair of the Self*. New York: W. W. Norton.

Siegel, D. J. (1999). *The Developing Mind*. New York: Guilford.

Slade, A., Sadler, L. & Mayes, L. C. (2005). Minding the baby: Enhancing parental reflective functioning in a nursing/mental health home visiting program. In: L. Berlin, Y. Ziv, L. Amaya-Jackson & M. Greenberg (Eds.), *Enhancing Early Attachments: Theory, Research, Intervention, and Policy* (pp. 152–177). New York: Guilford.

Slade, A., Sadler, L., de Dios-Kenn, C., Webb, D., Ezepchick, J. & Mayes, L. (2005). Minding the baby: A reflective parenting program. *Psychoanalytic Study of the Child, 60*: 74–100.

van der Kolk, B. (2006). Clinical implications of neuroscience research in PTSD. *Annals of New York Academy of Sciences, X*: 1–17.

Wachtel, P. (2008). *Relational Theory and the Practice of Psychotherapy*. New York: Guilford.

CHAPTER FIVE

States of terror and terrorist states: oppression and liberation in political and therapeutic contexts

Dick Blackwell

"If only it were all so simple. If only there were evil people somewhere insidiously committing evil deeds and it were necessary only to separate them from the rest of us and destroy them. But the line dividing good from evil cuts through the heart of every human being, and who is willing to destroy a piece of their own heart."[1]

—*Alexander Solzhenitsyn* (1974, p. 168)

"In psychoanalysis nothing is true except the exaggerations."[2]

—*Theodor Adorno* (1951, no. 29)

This chapter is based on my work with survivors of political oppression, most of whom have been refugees to the UK, mainly from what are commonly referred to as "third world" countries. It also draws on the observations about the contemporary social contexts in which we currently live, and on a range of individual and institutional responses to these contexts. I am concerned here not only with terrorised clients but with the ways in which we can ourselves individually and collectively become terrorised and can furthermore become terrorising.

Outline of philosophy of therapy

There are significant limitations to a model of therapy that has the therapist in a relatively healthy, well adjusted, well balanced position, well away from the edge; providing therapy/cure for a client who is in an extreme state close to the edge. While therapy is unarguably the attempt by the therapist to provide something helpful for the client, it is at the same time an encounter between persons in which both must confront extreme thoughts and feelings, and therapists too must address their own edges, their own capacities for fear, anxiety, rage, persecution. Therapy is in constant tension between the dynamics of the helping/ facilitating intention, and the shared existential encounter (Blackwell, 2007). It is also a struggle to find words to describe or express experience, and indeed to shape experience, and to experience what may be beyond words. So terms must be regarded always as somewhat problematic, and not taken too literally or concretely.

In work with refugees and survivors of political violence in the Third World, there has been a substantial critique of traditional diagnostic categories and modes of treatment. It has been argued that, in transposing the clinical discourses of one culture onto those of another, a form of cultural imperialism can take place, and that in implementing a solely clinical discourse on a political situation and on the consequences of political actions, a crucial loss or distortion of meaning takes place, with consequent alienation of both client and therapist (Bracken, 2002; Kordon et al., 1988; Summerfield, 1999, 2000). It is therefore important in the approach to therapy, to take account of not only the existential encounter between clients and therapists but also of the meaningful contexts of clients and therapists, and of the context of therapy itself.

Levels of context

I have previously argued for four levels of context to be taken account of in work with refugees: political, cultural, interpersonal, and intrapsychic. This provided a way of thinking about the context of individual identity (or fragmentation) and of individual and collective experience for both clients and therapists (Blackwell, 2005). I want to add economic and religious dimensions. I had previously included religion as part of culture, but it has become clear that religious belief can play such a powerful part in the lives of individuals and communities, not only as a source of conflict but as a source of comfort, survival, and recovery, that it needs to be thought of separately from culture. The economic dimension becomes increasingly important in recognising the impact of the lowly economic status, deprivation, and at times destitution that refugees experience in the UK which, along with the often present threat of deportation, serves to constitute states of continuing traumatic stress. These are also dimensions of the therapist's experience which we need to consider in addressing the relationships between therapists and clients.

States of terror in traumatised survivors

The following are some of the states of mind in which traumatised and terrorised clients present themselves. The list is not exhaustive, but serves to indicate the main areas we are concerned with.

It is worth keeping in mind the fact that the state of terror in the client's mind is not necessarily a legacy from a reality in the past, in another time and another place. The threat of failure of their asylum application, involving the threat of deportation back to the terror from which they have escaped, hangs contemporaneously over the heads of many of these clients. They thus exist in a continuing state of terror in the present.

The following list may be regarded to some extent as a list of emotions or experiences, as indeed they are. However, the value of thinking of them as states is that it conveys the sense of how powerful and captivating they are for the person experiencing them. An emotion is in the person, but the person is in the state.

Alienation—a sense of disconnection from others, of experiencing the world and oneself in a way so radically different as to set one apart from one's fellows, whether family, friends, colleagues, or fellow humans. There is difficulty making contact in therapy, and words seem inadequate. Therapists may have a sense that they are doing all the work and find themselves wondering why the client is coming.

Fear/terror/anxiety, whether of specific things (men in uniforms, men in general, fellow nationals) or states of high anxiety in which there appears to be no specific focus. The person may wake from a dream just terrified, feeling they are back in prison and unable to realise they are now in the UK. Some, who are victims of their own governments or communities, may fear anyone from their own country or ethnic group because they represent the persecutors.

Secrecy—this occurs particularly within families and between family members where it feels impossible to tell other family members what has been suffered or what is felt currently. Sometimes secrets have to be kept from the self too ... protection of each other.

Shame, and a sense of exposure or transparency, where it feels as if others will know or intuit a painful secret. So, to be seen by others is to experience humiliation. One of my colleagues, Gill Hinshelwood (1999a, 1999b) suggested that in this context, shame was often the key, or the gatekeeper, to other emotions or states, which was what stopped the rest being discussed. The perpetrators have done shameful things, but the victims carry the shame. This applies particularly to rape and other sexual violations. It may also relate to feelings of failure, either in relation to political causes or in relation to feelings of responsibility for friends and family. It is often linked to cultural beliefs and values but may also carry an existential transcultural component.

Fragmentation, where experiences cannot be remembered in a coherent narrative but only in bits and pieces with various gaps and disconnections. This is becoming an increasingly recognised reaction to trauma (Cohen, 2001; Herlihy & Turner, 2007), but it continues to pose problems for asylum applicants whose failure to provide a coherent and consistent account of their plight is often the basis for disbelief within the asylum system.

Dissociation, where events can be remembered and recounted without the emotion. Sometimes there seems to be a disconnection from the body or parts of it, especially where there are physical pains unexplained by medical examination. Extreme or generalised forms of this would seem to be what Lifton (1968), in his study of Hiroshima survivors, called "psychic numbing". This state can, to some extent, be engendered by having to tell the story for asylum applications. The story told in a therapeutic context can be told at a pace which is emotionally manageable, so that the emotions remain connected to and engaged with the memories. Where an account needs to be provided for other purposes and the pace is too fast for the emotional content to be managed, there is a need to disconnect the words from the feelings.

Survivor guilt—the feeling of not deserving to have survived when others have not. This can be particularly strong where it is other family members who have not survived.

Fear of overwhelming emotion in self and others—a sense that anger or sadness, or shame or other powerful feelings will be limitless, leading to destruction or drowning in tears. This fear contributes much to the protectiveness and secrecy often found in families.

Anger, frustration, rage, destructiveness, all of which may be feared because they are too close to the persecutory acts from which the victim has suffered. Disidentification with the aggressor is very important in some cases at some times, especially to recover some self-esteem and combat feelings of contamination, but it can also lead to denial of violent and aggressive feelings, which can then be turned against the self in depression and suicidal inclinations, and against the therapist and the therapy.

Dependency can be extreme. It is partly based on the reality of helplessness experienced at political, economic, and cultural levels, and on the psychological debilitation suffered as a result of traumatic experiences, which prevents effective functioning; and partly from a regression and transference which again operates at several levels, particularly intrapsychic and political, in which clients can seem to have regressed to quite infantile states. It has been said that, in trauma, the internal mother becomes a bystander, failing to intervene and protect. So this regression might be understood as an attempt to reactivate an external mother. There is also an internalisation of patterns of political and cultural dominance.

Despair and suicidal feelings. These may be related to the asylum situation and the fear/expectancy of being returned to the place of the original persecution. Such cases appear as an existential choice. Other cases involve feelings of being so damaged at various levels that there is no hope of restoring a life project or focus.

Faith and hope. I mention these, not because they are the results of traumatic or terrorising experiences, but because they are significant in what keeps many clients going, and provide a counterbalance to states of despair and suicide. They are states of mind that occur and provide sustenance and resilience in the context of terror. They are not concepts or ideas that are easy to define or describe, yet they nevertheless seem to be powerful and pervasive in some way or other. They can obviously be derived from religion, or politics, but may spring from a range of other sources. Many clients at the edge seem to exist in a state of tension between hope and faith on the one hand, and despair and hopelessness on the other. A substantial number report that they are kept from suicide only by the prohibition against it in their religion.

Faith and hope also have a place in the therapeutic encounter, of which I shall say more later.

States of terror in therapists and therapeutic teams

The above listed states of terror are to be found in traumatised victims of torture and political violence, but they can be readily projected into, picked up by, and resonated with, by therapists. Not only may they become internalised by individual therapists but they can get into therapeutic teams. A colleague described the distress felt by therapists at the poverty and material deprivation being suffered by so many of their clients as in effect terrorising them.

In my teams, too, intense feelings of helplessness arise in relation to clients' destitution, and the threat of deportation. These arouse powerful feelings of protectiveness towards the client, not only in relation to outside agencies but also in relation to colleagues perceived to be insufficiently supportive of the client.

Beyond this, other aspects of clients' states of terror can get into the therapists and their teams, and into their personal lives and interpersonal relationships. The anger/rage/violence/destructive conglomeration may be hardest to process in a context of striving to be helpful, collaborative, and empathic, and readily becomes the thing most dissociated from and most readily expressed in ways that are completely unrecognised. They may then be re-enacted in the therapeutic setting, both by individual therapists and by collective and institutional responses. Anger at clients can be expressed by neglect or impatience, or defended against by excessive helpfulness, or by depersonalisation in what may be described as professional detachment.

We are all vulnerable to these experiences, so reflection and recognition of these states and the different levels of context at which they can operate become important. I recall my co-therapist and I consulting a colleague about the conflicts we were experiencing in relation to a certain client family. Our colleague commented on one particularly violent and traumatic aspect of the family's experience and suggested that in the light of such horrors it was hardly surprising that we should be having some difficulties. Although this made no explicit connection between the clients' experiences and our conflict, it gave us a space to reflect on our feelings and the possibility that we were carrying something very powerful for our clients and that working on a regular basis with horrific events we were slow to recognise horror as "horror" and its impact on us.

It is important to recognise here the value of factors often overlooked in the professional discourse: faith, hope, love, and loyalty. Individuals and teams need faith and hope in the work they are doing and in the therapeutic relationship, along with bonds of attachment and loyalty to each other, in order to survive intact as effective teams. We also need to remember Solzhenitsyn's remark about the line between good and evil running through all of us, and to be prepared to pursue the exaggerations noted by Adorno (Jay, 1973).

Two tensions in the therapeutic encounter need to be worked with. The first is the tension between the helping relationship and the existential encounter. Sometimes a fellow human being sharing helplessness, impotence, and rage, and perhaps despair, may be more valuable and more real than a wise, thoughtful, and containing therapist, but not always! Containment and thought have vital parts to play as well.

The second tension is distance and relation. It is originally described by Buber (1957), and it was Robert Lifton (1979) who highlighted its relevance to work with "survivors". You need to step apart to relate. But not too far. You need detachment, but it does not go far without engagement. It is interesting to note in passing that some of the most creative reflection that I was able to do with a colleague was done over coffee in a local café. Inside the building in which we worked, our thinking seemed flooded and overwhelmed. It was only with the creation of a literal distance, the walk down the road to the café that it became possible to develop a more detached perspective.

However, detachment or distance can become problematic if it is disconnected from engagement or relation. It can be particularly problematic in organisations where some parts of the organisation are highly engaged and others quite detached. "Buffering" is a term I use to describe the ways that, in organisations dealing with highly distressed and frightening client populations, levels of hierarchy can function as buffers to protect those higher in the organisation, who are often central in determining its functioning and culture, from the levels of threat and anxiety to which front line staff are exposed. So, major decision-making is taking place in individually and collectively dissociated states of mind. At the same time those powerfully engaged with clients find a useful level of detachment or distance increasingly hard to achieve.

States of terror in populations

Some of these states of terror can be found in populations, both those living under overtly oppressive regimes, and those in allegedly democratic societies. They are more readily seen in overtly oppressive regimes, where secrecy, silence, dissociation, fear, fragmented perceptions and narratives, can be significant modes of survival, and perhaps the only ways of avoiding persecution. (See for example, Kordon et al. (1988), for an account of Argentina under military rule; and Havel (1987) on life in the old Soviet empire; and Melzak (1992) for a general view of the impact of such contexts on family life.) But in societies like our own, we see the sort of moral panics that can develop around, for example, asylum seekers, disorderly young people, or terrorist threats and we see particularly high levels of anxiety often accompanied by anger and rage, sometimes dissociated, against the particular problem group. We see these at different levels. Post 9/11 and 7/7 we see reactions from government and its institutions. Then there are media reactions and the feelings and anxieties of the population that both fuel, and feed off, the government and institutional responses. In less mainstream areas we might also interpret some of the "gang culture" and other forms of alienation among young people (such as homelessness, drug addiction, or prostitution) as violent responses to political, economic, and cultural contexts of despair and hopelessness, and a sense of institutionalised oppression. We can always argue about these matters, and I may be accused of exaggeration in comparing these states of individual and collective mind to those of survivors of torture and direct political violence. But I think it is more productive to operate on a continuum, where we can identify resonances between different societies and power structures and between different collections of individuals, than to allow categories to become encapsulated in hermetic discourses, in relation to which we can too easily and too readily dissociate ourselves. For example, the question came up in a presentation recently about the historical inaccuracy of the film *Mississippi Burning*. It occurs to me to raise the question as to whether the true historical picture was too overwhelming to be taken in, and the narrative had to be modified if not fragmented to make it bearable. Which raises a question about how much we fragment and modify our current narratives in order to have a "reality" we can live with and not be overwhelmed by.

Terrorist states of society and nation state

We begin to get, in the previous section, a sense of how a state of mind, which is the product of feeling terrorised, tips into a state of mind inclined to do some terrorising. It is worth considering the degree of popular support for at least the early stages of military repression in Argentina in the 1970s, and the level of support here in the UK for detention without trial, Guantanamo, and extraordinary rendition. We can also consider the levels of hostility to various stereotyped groups which I am sure it is unnecessary to list.

We might also want to include "bystanding" as a curious bridge between a state of terror and a terrorist state. It is important because it is the position in which so many people find themselves in relation to persecution and oppression. The components of terror, fear, anger, fragmented narratives, defences against guilt, dissociation from what is actually being done, etc., all play their parts in establishing bystander positions. But it is perhaps a small step from a bystander state of mind to a more persecutory way of thinking, moving towards a more terrorising inclination. Terrorist states of mind within a significant number of the population readily become terrorising actions of nation states.

In this context we can note certain terminological reversals that have an almost Orwellian quality. The term "terrorist" is most commonly applied to specific groups or organisations perceived as acting against legitimate governments and civil societies. These terrorist groups have no official political status: they are outlaws. But the historical reality is that most terrorism is enacted by governments. Colonialism was developed and maintained largely by violence and oppression against indigenous peoples. In the latter half of the twentieth century, the US led the world in supporting and facilitating military coups and oppressive and violent governments. It was often justified by the cold war but appears more primarily driven by the needs of economic and political elites and their need for global market conditions and ideological hegemony. The US government now claims leadership of a "war on terror". (See for example Chomsky, 1988, 1993.)

Asylum seekers who mainly come to this society as victims of oppression, seeking shelter and safety, come to be regarded as a threat. They will "swamp" the indigenous population, devour the resources of the welfare state, and subvert the existing society. Thus the smallest and most pathetic demands by the largely weak and helpless become subjected to labels far more appropriate to powerful transnational corporations, and the governments they support and are supported by.

These reversals themselves seem to rest, not only on splitting and projection and scapegoating, which we might recognise as familiar processes, but on forms of fragmentation of thought and narrative, where the whole historical story is too difficult, too horrifying, too "unbelievable" for it to be held in mind by individuals or groups. It therefore appears in fragments of history and ideology, accompanied often by high levels of dissociation defending against unbearable shame and guilt, and perhaps hopelessness.

We may also find high levels of dependency on government or other authority figures, which plays its part in facilitating gullibility to government pronouncements and media portrayals.

Terrorist states in organisations

Organisations in any society will to some extent reflect the hegemony of the ruling ideology, since neo-liberal economics and the terminology and values of the market place have permeated almost every level of organisational life, in both the public and private sectors. External demands and pressures will play their part. So, too, will the states of mind of those in power within the organisation and the states of mind of its members.

In organisations dealing with traumatised client groups, or traumatic situations, the "structural buffering" described earlier can facilitate a level of dissociation in senior managers and decision makers. Policies and procedures may then be implemented, and organisational cultures developed, which are substantially out of touch with, and ultimately undermining of, the actual work. Consequently, they become experienced as oppressive and, in a sense, terrorising for workers at lower levels of the organisation, particularly those at the front line, caught between what the clients bring and the requirements of the organisation (see, for example, policies on the management of suicide risks). I have encountered many staff in many organisations who feel a conflict between following their own professional judgement and following their organisation's procedures.

We then have the bizarre situation where terrorised clients are seeking help/therapy from staff who are themselves feeling terrorised by their own organisation, and probably by their own government, and perhaps unaware of how much they might be being terrorised by the clients. This encourages either overidentification with clients and concomitant loss of the necessary therapeutic distance, or a dissociation from the clients' experience and identification with the aggressor, in this case, the government and the organisation as represented by its managers and controllers.

Concluding remarks

My aim here has been not simply to address ways of doing "therapy at the edge" with a particular client group, nor primarily to map out, in psychosocial terms, the relationships between terror and terrorism, or between the terrorised state of mind, the terrorist state of mind, and terrorist or terrorising activity. My primary concern is to insist on the location of the former within the context of the latter. That is, we can only engage fully and meaningfully with states of terror in our clients when we can begin to recognise our own susceptibility to states of terror and terrorist states, in ourselves, our organisations, our communities, including our professional community, our society, and our governments.

I want to conclude with two final notes, one on power and the other on hope and faith.

In both, the reality of terror and the states of mind, power, and the seduction of power play a vital part. Oppression is the action of the powerful in exercising and maintaining their power. Terror maintains power. Power seeks the destruction of hope in those it oppresses. Hope is acceptable to power only on the terms that power dictates; and faith must be placed only in the powerful. That was the logic of the arms race and now seems to be the logic of the war against terror.

Hope and faith might be considered as opposites to power. They have to be placed in people and the potential of encounters between people. Yet we live now in an age where hope and faith are routinely placed in policies, procedures, governments, systems, and models: CBT, NICE, models of therapy, government regulation, user groups, speed cameras,

CCTV, ID cards, etc. Everywhere we find such attempts to police and control, as if we have lost faith in people and are engaged in a war against humanity itself, against ourselves and others. Although power may ultimately be a central problem, we place more and more faith in power and those in power. We can recall the high level of optimism engendered by the Blair election victory in 1997, a hope and faith in what might be done by power or those in power. In our work "empowerment" has become a vogue term, as if power is somehow virtuous rather than essentially problematic.

But hope and faith are essentially personal, interpersonal, and embedded in the complex dialectic between individuals and between individuals and their groups. The moving dialectic between therapists and clients can be located within this wider dialectic and is a place where the search for hope as an act of faith may be the primary quest from which the rest of the project develops. Organisations focused on the nurturing of hope and faith understood in this way may be more viable and less prone to terror and terrorising than those focused on such ideas as diagnosis, treatment, efficient service delivery, evaluation, etc. And if I may be permitted a wild hope, societies, and perhaps governments able to foster such a dialectic might be less susceptible to terror than those preoccupied with power and control.

Note

1. Reprinted by permission of HarperCollins Publishers Ltd @ 1974 Solzhenitsyn.
2. Reprinted by permission of the publisher, Verso.

References

Adorno, T. (1951). *Minima Moralia: Reflections on a Damaged Life*. London: Verso, 2005.
Blackwell, D. (2005). *Counselling and Psychotherapy with Refugees*. London: Jessica Kingsley.
Blackwell, D. (2007). Oppression and freedom in therapeutic space. *European Journal of Psychotherapy and Counselling*, 9(3): 255–265.
Bracken, P. (2002). *Trauma, Meaning and Philosophy*. London: Whurr.
Buber, M. (1957). Distance and relation. *Psychiatry*, 20: 77–104.
Chomsky, N. (1988). *The Culture of Terrorism*. London: Pluto Press.
Chomsky, N. (1993). *Year 501: The Conquest Continues*. London: Verso.

Cohen, J. (2001). Errors of recall and credibility: Can omissions and discrepancies in successive statements reasonably be said to undermine credibility of testimony. *Medico Legal Journal, 69*(1): 25–34.

Havel, V. (1987). *Living in Truth*. London: Faber and Faber.

Herlihy, J. & Turner, S. (2007). Memory and seeking asylum. *European Journal of Psychotherapy and Counselling, 9*(3): 267–276.

Hinshelwood, G. (1999a). Personal communication.

Hinshelwood, G. (1999b). Shame. The silent emotion. *Institute of Psychosexual Medicine Journal, 22*: 9–12.

Jay, M. (1973). *The Dialectical Imagination: A History of the Frankfurt School and the Institute for Social Research 1923–1950*. Boston: Little, Brown.

Kordon, D. R., Edelman, L. I., Lagos, D. M., Nicoletti, E., Bozzolo, R. C., Siaky, D., Host, M. L., Bonao, O. & Kersner, D. (1988). *The Psychological Effects of Political Oppression*. Buenos Aires, Argentina: Sudamericana Planeta.

Lifton, R. (1968). *Death in Life—Survivors of Hiroshima*. New York: Random House.

Lifton, R. (1979). Discussion following lecture: "On death and the Holocaust: Some thoughts on survivors", at The Survivor Syndrome Workshop, Institute of Group Analysis and Group Analytic Society.

Melzak, S. (1992). Secrecy, privacy, survival, repressive regimes and growing up. *Bulletin of the Anna Freud Centre, 15*: 205–224.

Solzhenitsyn, A. (1974). *The Gulag Archipelago 1918–1956*. London: Collins.

Summerfield, D. (1999). A critique of seven assumptions behind psychological trauma programmes in war affected areas. *Social Science and Medicine, 48*: 1449–1462.

Summerfield, D. (2000). Childhood war refugeedom and "trauma": Three core questions for mental health professionals. *Transcultural Psychiatry, 37*(3): 417–433.

CHAPTER SIX

Stepping into the void of dissociation: a therapist and a client in search of a meeting place*

Shoshi Asheri

The premise of this chapter is that when a client enters the therapy room bringing with them their traumatic experience, in whatever disorganised or dissociated, physiological and/or psychological manifestations, they inevitably enter into a relationship with a part of the therapist that would rather remain dissociated than feel the unbearable feelings that an engagement with such trauma can evoke, particularly if the therapist carries a related trauma of his or her own. If we accept this premise, an important and intriguing question arises: how do we negotiate a therapeutic meeting in the face of the unconscious pact between a therapist and a client to remain dissociated?

In order to explore this question I will relate a clinical experience in which my client's dissociated domestic trauma entered into a relationship with my dissociated political and personal trauma. What could have been a potentially re-traumatising re-enactment between two

---

*An original version of this chapter was presented as part of a plenary dialogue with Barbara Pizer at a CABP conference on "Relational Dilemmas and Opportunities" in September 2007 at Cambridge, UK. The theme of the dialogue was entitled "Negotiating a Sense of Aliveness in the Therapeutic Relationship: An Embodied Intersubjective Experience". That dialogue was the inspiration for this chapter.

people longing to be met, but remaining lost to each other in the void of their respective dissociations, became the key to a profound, mutually therapeutic, meeting.

> *1967. Israel. Jerusalem. I'm nine years old sitting in a shelter with my mother, my baby sister and our neighbours. It's now the second day of what will be called "The Six Day War". We can hear the warning sirens and the missiles falling intermittently above us. Some are clearly falling in our street. My baby sister is crying: we have run out of clean nappies. My mother seems helpless. "I'll run home and get some nappies," I say matter-of-factly. "Oh, OK," my mother replies.*
>
> *We live in a top floor flat across the road. I open the shelter's door and a strong smell of burning metal hits me ... I can see our flat on the other side of the road. I run across the road. I can hear the sirens going up and down, warning us again. "I've got to get these nappies," I tell myself, and run up the stairs to the top flat. I'm risking my life for a clean nappy. Neither my mother nor I seem to think much of this act.*

It took me decades before I began to question this moment of parenting; to consider that the maternal wasteland I found myself in, when offering my mother this crazy heroic act, could possibly be a traumatic event. I believe that this is an indication of the extent to which the intergenerational transmission of trauma through dissociation was the bread and butter of my upbringing. I grew up at a time when Israel as a nation was establishing what I would describe as a collective dissociation from fear and vulnerability following the trauma of the Holocaust and the ongoing threat to its survival.

Although these factors were exploited as justification for all political activities, the implicit and, at times, explicit message was, "It will never happen again because we'll make sure no cracks or weakness will be shown". Promotion of heroism, and a collective illusion of invincibility, protected my generation from the incomprehensible grief over the victims of the Holocaust, as well as the shameful and shockingly inappropriate feelings of contempt towards those victims who stepped into the gas chambers, although unknowingly, without a fight. The psychological and political positioning became one: becoming a victim to fear and vulnerability could not be an option ever again.

My parents, although left wing and peace seekers, were not immune to the collective mentality of promoting a tough exterior and negation of the terror within. I happened to be an intense seeker of emotional reality. They resolved my enquiries by becoming extremely liberal: "Feel free to think and do what you want, Shoshi, we trust your judgment". While my friends struggled with strict and overprotective boundaries, I had to deal with an expansive sense of freedom for which I was, and am still, deeply grateful. At the same time, I experienced a profound sense of aloneness when that limitlessness turned into an emotional wasteland where no holding or containing boundaries could be found.

You might wonder at this point why I am giving this personal story such prominence. Is my client's story not the subject of this clinical paper? I believe that when a client enters the therapy room, bringing with them their traumatic experience, they inevitably enter into a relationship with the part of me that embodies my personal and collective history. This part would rather remain dissociated than feel the unbearable feelings that an engagement with a trauma can evoke, even if my trained and conscious therapeutic position would claim otherwise. This presents a particular problem when both my client's and my own mechanism for coping with our respective traumas is dissociation.

Clearly, each therapeutic dyad holds its own particular relational matrix in relation to trauma and dissociation. However, I believe that there is a fundamental question that is likely to be relevant to all: to what extent can we undo the unconscious pact between therapist and client to remain dissociated, and what are the therapeutic positions and clinical tools that can help us to undo this unconscious pact?

Holding this question in mind, I would like to describe a clinical experience in which my client's dissociated domestic trauma entered into a relationship with my dissociated political and personal trauma. Both of us were unconsciously doing all that we could to remain dissociated until the therapeutic relationship ran into difficulties, which nearly ruptured the therapeutic alliance beyond repair. This could have been a painful and potentially re-traumatising re-enactment of two people longing to be met but remaining lost to each other in the void of their respective dissociations. Working on the edge of the void within us and between us, which can also be described as working on the edge of the conventional therapeutic frame, seemed at the time a necessary way forward.

But before I enter into the clinical case I want to give you one more necessary piece of personal information.

In the same period of time, with the backdrop of the political and personal atmosphere I described before, I developed a game—a very physical game. Across the road a new block of flats was being built. I used to sneak into the half-built building and run up to the first floor balcony. Looking down to the pile of sand the builders had left in the front, I would take my sandals off, catch the sense of the height and quickly jump. I landed on the pile of sand. I loved meeting my fear for one brief moment. I loved knowing just when to jump before it could take hold of me and I loved the sensation of the soft sand on my bare feet. "This is where my feet begin", I would say to myself, "and this is where my fear ends …". I would repeat the jump again and again until I mastered the moment, for long enough to feel the fear but not for it to take me over. And then there was the second floor. This was my ultimate thrill. Standing on the second floor balcony I realised I could not bypass my fear quickly enough. I had to stop and feel it. It was bigger than me. I would hold the edge of the balcony with my bare toes: can I do it? Dare I jump? Everything stopped except for my heartbeat. It was racing. I could feel the cold sweat running down my back. I could hear my breathing. Dare I? I had to stop and feel my fear. I found my edge. I found my limit. I could never be sure if I had it in me to cross the edge and leap into the void. Sometimes I did and sometimes I was just too scared. One might wonder if suicide was in my mind but to me it felt quite the opposite. In hindsight I believe that this was an attempt to feel a greater sense of aliveness. I believe that it was not only the thrill of flying or managing my fear that was so compelling to me. I believe that I needed to find my edge: the place where freedom and adventure meet danger and a need for discipline, the place where my limits became so tangible nobody, not even a whole nation, could overlook or deny its existence. In that moment of meeting my edge, the illusion of fearlessness and invincibility became undone. I was terrified. I was vulnerable and I could feel it running through my body. I felt naked of pretence and very much inside myself.

My client, whom I will call Tilli, came to me with severe anxiety and a general sense of deep exhaustion, which she knew was beyond a physical one. She had an obsessive need to wash herself before any potential touch. It had become a major issue in her long-term sexual partnership. No spontaneous touch could take place and, at times, even after washing herself she would withdraw just before or during lovemaking. Her partner, whom she loved very much and who had been tolerant for many years, was coming to the end of his acceptance. She loved her work as a counsellor in a school and was relieved that touch was not an option in the work context. For many months, our work together consisted of adult-to-adult conversations mainly focused on here and now issues to do with her relationship and her requirement that touch be predictable so she could wash beforehand. She shared her feelings and anxiety willingly and openly. There was a sense of us building a working alliance within an atmosphere of a warm and positive transference. I was aware, however, that she was very economical when it came to talking about her childhood and that I had to be particularly patient, spacious, and attuned to her internal rhythm in those moments.

About eighteen months into our work together, a change started to take place. Moments of silence between us grew bigger, Tilli started withholding her participation, my questions were met with a new evasiveness and gradually with a more outright defiance. "What do you mean there is a new feel to our session? What you get is what I feel, which is exactly what you got before", she said dismissively. When I attempted to enquire more, for example: "Tilli, we both know that what is happening between us now feels different from how it felt before", it sent her even further away. She felt more and more unreachable, punitive, and controlling and I felt more and more powerless. I tried to listen to the subtle tones of her withdrawal. Sometimes she felt to me like a sulky eight year old, at other times she felt like a disaffected cynical teenager, and occasionally she felt to me like a frightened and lost little girl—but that would never last long. It was as if she knew, on some level, that this part of her was her "weakest link" and could, potentially, be penetrated by me. This dynamic became much more challenging when I dared one day to try to give her a hand across the now painfully obvious barrier. I said, "Tilli, I can feel that you are trying to communicate something to me that I can only guess is unbearably painful". This sent her to a new level of defiant withholding, much more active, much more sadistic. Cutting, poking, and toxic sentences were thrown at me sideways and underhand. I felt teased, I felt played with, and, at times, I had an embodied experience of feeling as if I were being hit by stones, or pricked with sharp objects. I started having anxious recurrent dreams the night before our sessions. The dream images would vanish on waking and all that remained was a feeling of cold sweat and the face of my childhood friend Benny, so focused yet so far away.

I could not make much sense of it but I knew that I started to dread our sessions, in which I found myself pinned to my seat, like a paralysed rabbit caught in the headlights.

Tilli never missed a session and was never late. Experiencing her sadistic attacks, my masochistic receptiveness and my growing desire to retaliate became harder and harder to contain. In one session she said to me in her by now familiar dismissive tone, "You are also trained as a body psychotherapist. Aren't you supposed to hold me?" Very quickly, before I could allow any therapeutic consideration to catch me, I heard myself saying: "You must be joking ... there is nothing in me that wants to hold you right now. If anything, I want to put this big cushion between us, to protect myself from you and to protect you from me ..."

A first floor jump. An outrageous sentence from a therapist. We were both stunned. I could feel a different quality to her silence. Was there an opening? I felt as if there was nothing to lose. The jump had been done. I moved from my chair and sat leaning on the wall. I took the big cushion that was leaning on the mattress in my room and put it in front of me. I said: "Tilli, let's just do it. Let's have this cushion between us. Put yourself where you feel in relation to me". There was no hesitation. She came and sat with her back to me leaning on the cushion. Silent and defiant. From then on, there started an extraordinary process that still sends a shiver down my spine each time I think about it.

I want to draw attention for a moment to my internal process. As the familiar frozen silence sat between us I could feel glimpses of internal activity happening inside me. Sensations, images, half thoughts that I was trying hard to cover over and justify: "My client should be my focus, shouldn't she?" The internal pressure was growing. I had enough clinical experience to know that if necessary I could keep containing my internal activity as I had done so many times before. But what if ... what if today, in this session, I would follow my first floor jump by climbing up to the second floor? What would that mean right now in relation to Tilli and me? Hesitantly I climbed to the second floor searching for the edge of the balcony, using my bare feet to feel the ground. I collected all the clues, all the physical signs ... the sensations of sharp stones and sticks, the dream image of my friend Benny, so focused yet so far away ... My heart was racing ... my hands started sweating ... I knew in my body I was close to the edge. Can I? Dare I? Who will take care of Tilli when I am busy dropping over the edge and into myself? Who will hold her if I go somewhere I can hardly hold myself? Who would hold me? I was trying to gauge the pile of soft sand. Is it there? Can I trust it? My heart was running fast, I could hear my breathing and then …

> A few weeks after the Six Day War. Benny and me in the field behind our block of flats. His father, a high ranking officer in the army, whom he adored with all his might, never returned from the war. His body was never found. Weeks of silent waiting. Benny didn't talk to me any more. He'd give me instructions with his eyes and I knew what to do. One day Benny started torturing our neighbour's cat. He found a way to pin the cat down and he would poke it with any sharp object he could find. Stone and sticks. So focused. So silent. I was watching him, holding my tears back. Witnessing the tortured cat. Witnessing Benny's tortured soul. An unspoken pact between two nine year olds was set up between us. "Lo mesaprim." "This should never be spoken about."

Tears from long-held silences gathered up in my eyes and as I felt the tender flow run down my face, I felt myself with Tilli who was sitting with her back to me, leaning on the big cushion. I tightened my holding around the cushion, without touching her in any way (Asheri, 2008), probably to anchor myself, yet, at the same time to communicate to her with no spoken words: "You jump too, Tilli, I'm here. I'm here like I haven't been able to be here before".

Her breathing was changing. I could see her back trembling. I could sense the release of her tears. Silent tears. "It's unbearable isn't it?" I whisper. Words I had heard myself say to her before with genuine empathy but not like this. Not from deep inside myself. Not from deep inside my body. A sound burst out of her, like a howling animal. She was sobbing now … and then words followed. … She was eight. Her two cousins, thirteen and fifteen, came to visit every other Sunday for afternoon tea. They were sent to play in the woods behind the house. Each visit, the two of them would take turns. One of them would pin her down while the other would use anything they could find, sharp stones and sticks, to pursue their sexual activity. … The three of them would come back into the house at four o'clock to have their tea and cakes with Tilli's mum and aunt. Nobody said anything. Nobody asked any questions, not even when Tilli disappeared for a long time to clean herself. Even her recurrent vaginal infection did not bring questions.

Our sessions continued for many weeks in this position, with Tilli sitting with her back to me, leaning on the big cushion which was between us absorbing our separateness as well as our connection. Many more details of her sexual abuse unravelled. She wanted "every scrap of it out" she said. One day in the middle of the session she said, "Today, I can imagine touching your hand without having to wash myself first". I gently moved the cushion away. Tilli turned herself and faced me.

There are many ways we can discuss the mystery as well as the neuroscience of the unconscious, subliminal, right brain to right brain communication which featured so largely in our therapeutic process. However, what I would like to focus on is my understanding of the relational matrix that our respective dissociations faced us with, and the nature of my therapeutic positioning and the clinical tools I used.

In this paper I refer to dissociation in accordance with the contemporary psychoanalytic understanding of the dissociative process as the mind organising the traumatic memories by splitting them off from associative accessibility. In Bromberg's (1998) words: "Dissociation, the disconnection of the mind from the psyche-soma, then becomes the most adaptive solution to preserving self-continuity" (p. 273). Davies and Frawley (1992), in their description of the dissociative processes of adult survivors of childhood sexual abuse, emphasise that rather than the memories being repressed and forgotten, the child develops other modes of functioning, other adaptive self-states that co-exist on a continuum and alternate in mutually exclusive patterns, thus protecting the core of the wounded and abandoned child. Davies and Frawley suggest that, in making contact with the split off, dissociated child within the adult, we free the old objects to work their way into the transference–countertransference dynamic. Hence, the clinical question as they see it "is not what is conscious and what is unconscious, but rather, what is available and conscious in the patient at a particular point in time and what clinical interventions best serve the purpose of integration" (p. 7).

Although I agree that this is the important clinical question, what I believe needs to follow is an intriguing and a necessary question that takes into account the possible relationship between the client's process of dissociation and the therapist's process of dissociation as they interact consciously and unconsciously in the "here and now". In other words, we need to ask ourselves: what is the connection between what is conscious and available to the client at a particular point in time and what is conscious and available to the therapist at the same time? More specifically: how do we go about negotiating a therapeutic meeting when both client and therapist would rather stay within their safety zone by deadening their availability to become conscious of what is uncomfortable and, at times, traumatic?

Going back to my clinical example, as I understand it, Tilli's memories of her sexual abuse were not repressed or forgotten before she disclosed them to me but, rather, split off in order to protect and preserve the state of her internal world and the continuity of her sense of self. When she felt held enough by our working alliance, her hurting, raging, and abandoned child entered into the room long before her disclosure of sexual abuse. A detailed exploration of the sadomasochistic dynamic, where the positions of abused, abuser, and rescuer were like shifting sand between us while working their way through the transference and countertransference, is beyond the scope of this chapter. However, suffice to say that her embodied, yet dissociated experience of being sadistically played with, invaded, and ultimately tortured, triggered one of the painful and shameful experiences in my history. We shared a similar desperate investment to keep our respective experiences dissociated and unavailable to our consciousness. Paradoxically, we both shared a desperate longing for our story, our wound, to be known and recognised. I understand my initial, first floor jump intervention of, "You must be joking, nothing in me wants to hold you now. In fact I want to put this big cushion between us to protect myself from you and you from me", as being what Barbara Pizer (2005, p. 14) might describe as "outrageous intervention". In her paper, Pizer talks about a therapeutic process in which aspects of her mind, held largely in dissociation, were evoked by her intuitive awareness of dissociated or stuck aspects of her patient's mind. As a result of this "accidental" meeting of dissociated minds she developed a theoretical concept that she named "an outrageous interpretation": meaning, as she says, "an intervention that serves neither to clarify nor to contain but rather to connect with affective energy a dissociated space in the analyst, mobilized by the analyst's apperception of a dissociated space within the patient" (p. 14). She explains that an "outrageous interpretation" is a response that originates from a place within the therapist that is shut down by a history of intense shame over her affective responses and is evoked by the client's dissociated material. From the shut down place the therapist produces a communication of sufficient emotional intensity and evocativeness to enter a place in the client that is similarly shut down, so the client may regain a state of presence and emotional experience.

As I understand it, in my "first floor jump" intervention, I was led by an intuitive hunch based on no rational data and stemming from my own history, where, on some embodied yet not fully conscious level, I recognised a frightened child behaving "tough" and omnipotent, yet desperate for someone to hold a clear boundary and say, "Stop now. You are hurting yourself as well as me". Moreover, this spontaneous response was followed by a "second floor intervention" where I embarked on a very risky yet carefully considered therapeutic process. This "second floor intervention" was based on the premise that we protect and preserve ourselves by developing familiar, predictable patterns and habitual ways of being and relating. Our wounds and vulnerabilities, particularly the most unbearable ones, are hovering beyond the edge of this safety zone. As therapists we do something similar, we develop predictable therapeutic ways of relating which sit safely within well-argued theoretical frames, which are coloured by our countertransference reactions to our personal history (including our traumas) as well as our transference towards our trainers, supervisors, or thinkers in our professional field. However, some clients take us to the edge of what feels safe or even legitimate to us professionally and, at times, personally. In order to facilitate therapeutic change with those clients, in order to integrate what we would rather keep dissociated, I believe we need to require of ourselves what we require of our clients: to stand on the edge of our comfort zone and be prepared to step outside it by dropping down into our vulnerability in order to reach through the void of our dissociation. I believe that, if the therapy is to be effective, it is not enough to do it in the privacy of our personal therapy and supervision. Our clients need to *experience* us doing it, have a *felt sense* of it happening in the intersubjective space. By having an embodied sense of us dropping into our vulnerability and surrendering ourselves to ourselves, the mutual therapeutic impact comes to life and they can have the *experiential knowledge* of being recognised in their woundedness as well as recognising the other's wound. They, and we, find ourselves participating in a new reality, which we co-create and which changes us as we engage.

The obvious question is: who is holding the therapeutic responsibility in that moment? Are we burdening our clients with our own material?

Although the therapeutic process in such moments may seem to have a flavour of mutual regression, I have no doubt that the asymmetry of the power responsibility can and must remain intact. When Tilli's distressed child unconsciously evoked my distressed child and my distressed child, with no spoken words, invited, in return, Tilli's distressed child to have a voice, other self states in me were operating simultaneously. The adult in me, the therapist, the mother I wish I had had, were all holding the distressed children involved— Tilli's abused child and my wounded child. In other words, when I stepped into the void of my own material another part of me held on to my therapeutic responsibility although, admittedly, at moments only by a thread, and took care of both of us. I knew I had not lost my grip on the therapeutic relationship. On the contrary, a part of me sensed that my dropping down into the danger of my dissociation was *required*, for my edge to come in contact with hers, for me to invite her non-verbally, by example, to surrender to the traumatic pain of the past in order to live more fully in the present and truly contemplate a future. Moreover, I believe that it was not only I who took care of the two distressed children, it was, also, the fine tapestry of the relationship between us, which we had woven so delicately, so devotedly together over the long-term journey we had been engaged in. Going back to my metaphor of the "soft sand", what I was landing on was not, in any way, my client, but the combination of *my ethical and responsible self as well as the safety net of the intersubjective space* which we co-created over time.

Now, how do I assess that this intersubjective safety net is safe? As Karen Maroda (2002) put it:

> Patients do not regress and surrender on their own. It is up to us whether we fight them in this process or whether we willingly participate. However, the same rules apply to our patients. We do not give over to people we perceive as dangerous; we give over as part of a long-term relationship ... *Mutual surrender is a relational achievement, not a given.* (p. 56, my emphasis)

In summary, Hesse and Main (2000), in their discussion about emotional difficulties systematically associated with disorganised attachment, suggest that clinicians who are puzzled by the distressed behaviour of patients manifesting in catastrophic fantasies, long silences, and/ or attempts to control the clinician through punitive or inappropriate solicitous behaviour, may at times need to consider that the patient's behaviour is rooted in early responses to the "real" experiences of caregivers. What I have tried to demonstrate is that, at times, it is not only the client's caregiver's "real" experience that may be affecting the therapeutic relationship but also the *therapist's* "real" experience. Moreover, the therapeutic meeting between these two wounded people, who unconsciously would rather remain dissociated from their pain, can easily result in non-meeting or mutual misrecognition as Jessica Benjamin (1990) might describe it. However, the respective wounds which most likely brought them together in the first place (the wound that brought the client into therapy and the wound that drove the therapist to become a therapist) also hold the potential for mutual healing and mutual recognition.

What makes the difference between the possibility of therapist and client meeting each other or missing each other?

I can identify three important conditions related to the therapist's position:

1. The therapist's willingness to acknowledge and experience that there are *two* wounded people sitting in the room (not to be confused with disclosure).
2. The therapist's willingness not only to engage with the complexity of the transference/countertransference inherent in this situation, but to be guided by the client's need for the therapist to *participate* in the relational matrix that is emerging from the process. For example, to include work not only with the dissociated child which is within the client but also *internal* work with the dissociated child which is within the therapist, as this may be an essential vehicle for reaching the client's unconscious material.
3. The therapist's willingness to stretch her psychological and professional agility by allowing one self state to step off the edge of the therapeutic frame into the intrapsychic and intersubjective experience, while another self state is holding on to the frame of therapeutic reflection and responsibility.

There is no question that this is a very delicate, very complex, and very risky process where things can, and do, go awry. Many times, there will be inevitable re-enactments that can become essential to the therapeutic process if we manage to use them therapeutically. However, there are probably some particular clinical tools we may need to develop in our psychotherapeutic training in order to guide and monitor this kind of work. We need, for example:

- To put more emphasis and value in our training on the unconscious emergence of spontaneity, the "felt sense" and the "wisdom of the body", the right brain to right brain communication and intersubjective co-regulation between therapist and client, and use these as signposts that can guide us to the hidden narrative.
- To put more emphasis and value in our training on the therapist's *embodied* awareness of where his or her comfort zone ends and an *embodied* sense of where the therapist's personal and professional risk zone begins.
- To put more emphasis and value on recognising and embodying the ebb and flow of the relational charge and the ability to tolerate the aliveness, as well as the discomfort, it may evoke.
- To become trained to ask ourselves, moment by moment, "How is this client's bodymind story impacting on my bodymind story? For example: am I about to risk dropping off the edge because my habitual bodymind pattern is to drop off edges when I can't tolerate the powerlessness of making no impact on my client? Or am I about to drop off the edge because my client and I are getting comfortable in the painful impasse we are in and the true discomfort is in the places we seem to deaden or dissociate from? In short, is my risky intervention going to take us *into* a more real engagement or *out* of it?"

Finally, it is clear that this way of working chimes with the modern neuroscientific notion that sees the main therapeutic agent for change not in insight and cognition but in right brain to right brain communication within the attachment relationship. However, while neuroscientists usually research and observe the subjectivity of our inner world and the intersubjectivity of the social-relational world, we psychotherapists are called to get involved and participate in a risky endeavour which requires that we rub against our wounds and vulnerability on a daily basis. Why are we really choosing to do it?

All I can say for myself is that when Tilli and I managed to have our unspoken "accidental meeting", through daring to drop into the void of our respective dissociations, a key reorganisation took place. For a moment our secret yet shared lifelong relational assumption that *"we are utterly on our own in an emotional wasteland"* was challenged. For one exquisite moment we sensed and felt "another" coming to meet us in recognition.

Going back to the war zone I came from, as you can imagine, this is also my deepest political wish for the two sides involved. If I had to put my wish in one sentence and risk sounding politically naïve, I would say: may both sides dare to move from mutely terrorising to mutually recognising past and present terror and thus allow the possibility of meeting in the middle of their internal and external land.

References

Asheri, S. (2008). To touch or not to touch: A relational body psychother-apy perspective. In: L. Hartley (Ed.), *Contemporary Body Psychotherapy*. London: Routledge.

Benjamin, J. (1990). Recognition and destruction—an outline of intersubjec-tivity. In: S. A. Mitchell & L. Aron (Eds.), *Relational Psychoanalysis—The Emergence of a Tradition*. Hillsdale, NJ: The Analytic Press, 1999.

Bromberg, P. M. (1998). *Standing in the Spaces*. Hillsdale, NJ: The Analytic Press.

Davies, J. M. & Frawley, M. G. (1992). Dissociative processes and transference–countertransference paradigms in the psychoanalytically oriented treatment of adult survivors of childhood sexual abuse. *Psycho-analytic Dialogues*, 2(1): 5–36.

Hesse, E. & Main, M. (2000). Disorganised infant, child, and adult attachment: Collapse in behavioural and attentional strategies. *Journal of the American Psychodynamic Association*, 48(4): 1097–1127.

Maroda, K. J. (2002). *Seduction, Surrender, and Transformation*. Hillsdale, NJ: The Analytic Press.

Pizer, B. (2005). "Eva Get the Goldfish Bowl": Affect and intuition in the analytic relationship. [Invited Paper Presentation: Toronto Institute for Contemporary Psychoanalysis.]

Reading list

Books

Allen, J., Als, H., Lewis, J. & Litwack, L. F. (2008). *Without Sanctuary: Lynching Photography in America*. Santa Fe, NM: Twin Palms.

Bergmann, M. V. (1982). Thoughts on superego pathology of survivors and their children. In: M. S. Bergmann & M. Jucovy (Eds.), *Generations of the Holocaust*. New York: Columbia University Press, 1990.

Bizos, G. (1998). *No One to Blame? In Pursuit of Justice in South Africa*. Cape Town, South Africa: David Philip/Mayibuye.

Blackwell, D. (2005). *Counselling and Psychotherapy with Refugees*. London: Jessica Kingsley.

Bloom, S. (1997). *Creating Sanctuary: Toward the Evolution of Sane Societies*. London: Routledge.

Breger, L. (2000). *Freud: Darkness in the Midst of Vision*. Chichester: Wiley.

Bromberg, P. M. (2001). *Standing in the Spaces: Essays on Clinical Process, Trauma and Dissociation*. New York: Analytic Press.

Busch, F. (Ed.) (2008). *Mentalization: Theoretical Considerations, Research Findings, and Clinical Implications*. New York: Analytic Press.

Cameron, J. (1994). *A Time of Terror*. Baltimore: Black Classics Press.

Cohen, S. (2001). *States of Denial: Knowing about Atrocities and Suffering*. Cambridge: Polity Press.

Fletchman Smith, B. (2000). *Mental Slavery: Psychoanalytic Studies of Caribbean People*. London: Rebus Press.

Freud, S. (1919d). Introduction to psycho-analysis and the war neuroses. *S. E.*, *17*: 205–210. London: Hogarth.

Gerhardt, S. (2004). *Why Love Matters: How Affection Shapes a Baby's Brain*. London: Routledge.

Grossman, D. (1991). *See Under: Love*. London: Pan.

Herman, J. (1992). *Trauma and Recovery: The Aftermath of Violence from Domestic Abuse to Political Terror*. New York: Basic.

Hesse, E., Main, M., Abrams, K. Y. & Rifkin, A. (2003). Unresolved states regarding loss or abuse can have "second-generation" effects: Disorganized, role-inversion and frightening ideation in the offspring of traumatized non-maltreating parents. In: D. J. Siegel & M. F. Solomon (Eds.), *Healing Trauma: Attachment, Mind, Body and Brain* (pp. 57–106). New York: W. W. Norton.

Kogan, I. (1995). *The Cry of Mute Children*. London: Free Association.

Krystal, H. (Ed.) (1968). *Massive Psychic Trauma*. New York: International Universities Press.

Lyon, D. (1992). *Memories of the Southern Civil Rights Movement*. London: University of North Carolina Press.

Marable, M., Mullings, L. & Spencer-Wood, S. (2006). *Freedom: A Monumental Visual Record of African American History since the 19th Century*. London: Phaidon Press.

Payne, C. M. (1995). *I've Got the Light of Freedom*. Berkeley, CA: University of California Press.

Read, J., Mosher, L. R. & Bentall, R. P. (Eds.) (2004). *Models of Madness: Psychological, Social and Biological Approaches to Schizophrenia*. London: Routledge.

Sinason, V. (2002). *Attachment, Trauma and Multiplicity: Working with Dissociative Identity Disorder*. London: Brunner-Routledge.

Slade, A. & Wolf, D. P. (Eds.) (1994). *Children at Play*. Oxford: Oxford University Press.

Solomon, J. & George, C. (1999). *Attachment Disorganization*. New York: Guilford.

Stapley, L. (2006). *Globalisation and Terrorism*. London: Karnac.

Turner, J., Stanton, B., Vahala, M. & Williams, R. (1982). *The Ku Klux Klan, a History of Racism and Violence*. Klanwatch, a project of The Southern Poverty Law Center, Montgomery, AL.

van der Hart, O., Nijenhuis, E. R. S. & Steele, K. (2006). *The Haunted Self: Structural Dissociation and the Treatment of Chronic Traumatization*. New York: W. W. Norton.

van der Kolk, B. A., McFarlane, A. C. & Weisaeth, L. (1996). *Traumatic Stress: The Effects of Overwhelming Experience on Mind, Body, and Society.* New York: Guilford.

Wardi, D. (1992). *Memorial Candles: Children of the Holocaust.* (International Library of Group Psychotherapy.) London: Routledge.

Werbart, A. & Lindbom-Jakobson, M. (2001). The "living dead"—survivors of torture and psychosis. In: P. Williams (Ed.), *A Language for Psychosis: Psychoanalysis of Psychotic States.* London: Whurr.

Zulueta, de F. (2006). *From Pain to Violence: The Roots of Human Destructiveness.* Chichester, UK: Wiley.

Journals and journal articles

European Journal of Psychotherapy and Counselling, 9(3), September 2007—Special Issue: Refugees and Asylum Seekers, Eds. Rachel Tribe and Andrew Keefe.

Hesse, E. (1996). Discourse, memory and the adult attachment interview: A note with emphasis on the emerging cannot classify category. *Infant Mental Health Journal, 17*: 4–11.

Hesse, E. & Main, M. (2000). Disorganized infant, child and adult attachment: Collapse in behavioral and attentional strategies. *Journal of the American Psychoanalytic Association, 48*: 1097–1127.

Read, J., Van Os, J., Morrison, A. P. & Ross, C. A. (2005). Childhood trauma, psychosis and schizophrenia: A literature review with theoretical and clinical implications. *Acta Psychiatrica Scandinavica, 112*: 330–350.

Introduction to The Bowlby Centre

Promoting attachment and inclusion

Since 1976 The Bowlby Centre (formerly known as CAPP) has developed as an organisation committed to the practice of attachment-based psychoanalytic psychotherapy. The Bowlby Centre is a dynamic, rapidly developing charity which aims both to train attachment-based psychoanalytic psychotherapists and to deliver a psychotherapy service to those who are most marginalised and frequently excluded from long term psychotherapy.

We provide a four year part-time psychotherapy training accredited by the UKCP and operate a psychotherapy referral service for the public including the low cost Blues Project. The Bowlby Centre has a wealth of experience in the fields of attachment and loss and particular expertise in working with trauma and abuse. As part of our ongoing commitment to anti-discriminatory practice we offer a consultation service to the public and private sectors and are engaged in outreach and special projects working with care leavers, women experiencing violence and abuse, offenders and ex-offenders, people struggling with addiction to drugs, alcohol, eating difficulties or self-harm, and to individuals and groups in a wide variety of mental health settings.

We run short courses on "Attachment and Dissociation", and "The Application of Attachment Theory to Clinical Issues" including learning disabilities. The Bowlby Centre organises conferences including the annual John Bowlby Memorial Lecture, and has a series of publications which aim to further thinking and development in the field of attachment.

Bowlby Centre members participate extensively in all aspects of the field, making outstanding theoretical, research, and clinical contributions. Their cutting edge work is consistently published in the leading journals and monographs.

The Bowlby Centre values

- The Centre believes that mental distress has its origin in failed and inadequate attachment relationships in early life and is best treated in the context of a long-term human relationship.
- Attachment relationships are shaped in the real world and impacted upon by poverty, discrimination, and social inequality. The impact of the social world will be part of the therapy.
- Psychotherapy should be available to all, and from an attachment-based psychoanalytic perspective, especially those discriminated against or described as "unsuitable" for therapy.
- Psychotherapy should be provided with respect, warmth, openness, a readiness to interact and relate, and free from discrimination of any kind.
- Those who have been silenced about their experiences and survival strategies must have their reality acknowledged and not pathologised.
- The Bowlby Centre values inclusiveness, access, diversity, authenticity, and excellence. All participants in our organisation share the responsibility for anti-discriminatory practice in relation to race, ethnicity, gender, sexuality, age, (dis)ability, religion, class, and educational and learning style.

Patrons

Sir Richard Bowlby
Dr Elaine Arnold

Trustees

Brian Ryerkirk
Dick Blackwell
Janie Harvey-Douglas
Jeremy Rutter

For more information please contact:

The Bowlby Centre
147 Commercial Street
Spitalfields
London El 6BJ.
Telephone: 020 7247 9101
Email: admin@thebowlbycentre.org.uk
www.thebowlbycentre.org.uk

INDEX

For Product Safety Concerns and Information please contact our EU
representative GPSR@taylorandfrancis.com Taylor & Francis Verlag GmbH,
Kaufingerstraße 24, 80331 München, Germany

Batch number: 08153793

Printed by Printforce, the Netherlands